IN FOCUS 1

A vocabulary-driven, multi-skills critical thinking course

JN126077

Charles Browne • Brent Culligan • Joseph Phillips

KINSEIDO

Kinseido Publishing Co., Ltd.
3-21 Kanda Jimbo-cho, Chiyoda-ku,
Tokyo 101-0051, Japan

Copyright © 2024 by Charles Browne
                  Brent Culligan
                  Joseph Phillips

First published 2024 by Kinseido Publishing Co., Ltd.

Book and cover design SunCross Media LLC

Contents

Plan of the book

Research skills	Writing	Critical thinking	
		Skills	Speaking
Information gathering • Analyzing advertisements Comparing results • Comparing and discussing advertisements and their effectiveness	Keyword sentence writing The most popular and effective advertising techniques Writing a short social media post	Matching statements with the author's opinion Categorizing the effects of advertising: positive or negative	Discussion • Matching slogans with advertising techniques • Greenwashing as an advertising technique Quotable Quotes • Discussing whether advertising must always tell the truth
Information gathering • Matching advertisements with advertising technique Comparing results • Comparing and discussing advertising techniques and their popularity	Keyword sentence writing Pros and cons of advertising Writing a short social media post	Matching statements with the author's opinion Ranking personal information that students are willing to provide online	Discussion • Designing an online ad • Presenting the ad to the class and agreeing which is most effective Quotable Quotes • Discussing the power of advertising to influence people
Information gathering • Ranking how dangerous certain sports are Comparing results • Comparing and discussing popularity of sports	Keyword sentence writing Taking up a sport again after a serious accident Writing a short social media post	Matching statements with the author's opinion Finding out and ranking the reasons for people to do sports	Discussion • Should extreme athletes have to pay their own hospital bills? Quotable Quotes • Discussing people who live dangerously
Information gathering • Collecting information on real cases of competition Comparing results • Comparing and discussing other cases of real-world competition	Keyword sentence writing Should dangerous or risky activities be a question of personal choice? Writing a short social media post	Matching statements with the author's opinion Ranking activities in which drugs are likely to be used	Discussion • Where and how people compete in life Quotable Quotes • Discussing how important winning is
Information gathering • Comparing the average age of populations in different countries Comparing results • Comparing ideas for coping with different population ages	Keyword sentence writing What old people fear most about growing old Writing a short social media post	Matching statements with the author's opinion Ranking fears about old age	Discussion • Considering questions about society and the elderly Quotable Quotes • Discussing the best age to be rich and poor
Information gathering • Ranking time spent on everyday activities in the UK Comparing results • Comparing and discussing the results with those of students	Keyword sentence writing Issues and disadvantages of living very long lives Writing a short social media post	Matching statements with the author's opinion Ranking lifestyles that lead to a long life	Discussion • Planning life after retirement • Presenting plans to the class Quotable Quotes • Discussing the meaning of quality of life

Plan of the book

Unit	Title	Reading texts	Reading skills	Vocabulary	Listening
7 pp. 49–56	Robots in the Home	1 Living with Robots 2 A New Member of the Family	Skimming Scanning Identifying topic and main idea Identifying unnecessary information Identifying opinions	Identifying a part of speech: nouns Word parts: *uni* Example: *universal*	Discussion dictation Listen to readings online
8 pp. 57–64	I Lost my Job to a Machine	1 Technology and Society 2 The New Luddites?	Skimming Scanning Identifying topic and main idea Identifying unnecessary information Identifying opinions	Words in context Word parts: *auto* Example: *automobile*	Discussion dictation Listen to readings online
9 pp. 65–72	Animals: Our Research Partners?	1 Animal Testing 2 Is Animal Research Necessary?	Skimming Scanning Identifying topic and main idea Logical reasoning Identifying opinions	Word friends (collocations) Word parts: *dis* Example: *disease*	Discussion dictation Listen to readings online
10 pp. 73–80	Treatment of Animals	1 Standing Up for Animals 2 People for Animal Rights	Skimming Scanning Identifying topic and main idea Logical reasoning Identifying opinions	Words in context Word parts: *sub* Example: *subzero*	Discussion dictation Listen to readings online
11 pp. 81–88	Online (Dis)Information	1 The Shift to Large Language Models 2 Our Smart Best Friends	Skimming Scanning Identifying topic and main idea Finding supporting ideas Identifying opinions	Word friends (collocations) Word parts: *sur* Example: *survey*	Discussion dictation Listen to readings online
12 pp. 89–96	News: Fact or Fake?	1 Online Information: A Brief History 2 Misinformation Highways	Skimming Scanning Identifying topic and main idea Finding supporting ideas Identifying opinions	Words in context Word parts: *inter* Example: *internet*	Discussion dictation Listen to readings online

| Research skills | Writing | Critical thinking | |
		Skills	Speaking
Information gathering • Completing an information chart on movies starring robots Comparing results • Discussing different functions of robots and which types will exist in the future	Keyword sentence writing Should robots have rights? Writing a short social media post	Matching statements with the author's opinion Ranking household activities that robots could do	Discussion • Designing a new robot in a small group • Presenting the robot to the class Quotable Quotes • Discussing whether data on computers is safe
Information gathering • Brainstorming areas where robots can replace humans Comparing results • Discussing jobs that robots should not do	Keyword sentence writing Pros and cons of technology and society Writing a short social media post	Matching statements with the author's opinion Ranking likelihood of jobs for robots in the future	Discussion • Discussing probable, possible, and impossible technological inventions Quotable Quotes • Discussing the role of the teacher and technology in the classroom
Information gathering • Completing an information chart on animals and medical research Comparing results • Discussing the use of animals to find cures for diseases	Keyword sentence writing Reacting to opinions on the use of animals in research Writing a short social media post	Matching statements with the author's opinion Ranking which animals should have most rights	Discussion • Assessing different arguments for and against animal rights • Deciding as a class who wins the vote Quotable Quotes • Discussing whether cosmetics could be tested on prisoners
Information gathering • Collecting information on food production in different countries Comparing results • Comparing and discussing the results	Keyword sentence writing Should protesters be allowed to stop a circus performance? Writing a short social media post	Matching statements with the author's opinion Ranking animals from most liked to least liked	Discussion • Discussing different opinions on the treatment of animals Quotable Quotes • Discussing quotes for and against killing animals
Information gathering • Questionnaire on internet media usage by students Comparing results • Comparing and discussing popularity of media usage	Keyword sentence writing Pros and cons of using LLMs to do research on the internet Writing a short social media post	Matching statements with the author's opinion Ranking different news sources	Discussion • The right to use information available on the internet • Reporting results of discussions Quotable Quotes • Discussing AI and its effect on humanity
Information gathering • Matching headlines to category of news story Comparing results • Finding out which news stories are most popular	Keyword sentence writing Very unusual news stories Writing a short social media post	Matching statements with the author's opinion Ranking how probable different news stories are	Discussion • Discussing the differences between traditional reporting and citizen journalism • Reporting ideas to the class Quotable Quotes • Discussing if the media can control the way people think

Acknowledgments

Charles Browne would like to thank his wife, Yukari, and their three children, Joshua, Noah, and Hannah.

Joseph Phillips would like to acknowledge the support of his family.

Brent Culligan would like to thank his family in Japan and Canada who provided the motivation to take on this project.

The authors would like to thank Richard Walker for his tireless, patient, and positive support throughout the entire writing process.

The authors would also like to thank the entire Kinseido team for their faith in this exciting new chapter in the life of the *In Focus* series, especially Masato Fukuoka, Takahiro Imakado, Kyuta Sato and Alastair Lamond.

Kinseido and the authors appreciate Christopher Wenger and Brian Romeo of SunCross Media for their valuable design contributions.

To the teacher

Welcome to *In Focus*, a multi-level, corpus-informed course aimed at high school and university students. *In Focus* is designed to build all four skills, while also systematically developing knowledge of core vocabulary and students' critical thinking skills. Each Student Book contains 12 topic-based units, which are divided into six general themes. It provides two units in a row on each theme to help better develop students' critical thinking skills on these issues.

In Focus is supplemented by a range of free online learning components, which provide great flexibility and help to speed language acquisition.

We have created a unique lexical syllabus containing the most important words for second language learners of English. The authors of this series are also the creators of the New General Service List Project (www.newgeneralservicelist.com), a collection of corpus-based word lists, each providing the highest coverage in the world for that specific genre. The syllabus for *In Focus 1* is based on the New General Service List (NGSL), a list of approximately 2,800 words that allows them to understand approximately 92 percent of the words in most texts of general English. These are nearly all the words learners will ever need (not bad, if you consider there are more than 600,000 words in English!). In each level of *In Focus*, 120 of these words are taught in depth (10 per unit). In *In Focus 1* and *In Focus 2*, these words are taken from the NGSL, while in *In Focus Academic 1*, they are taken from the New Academic Word List (NAWL). Students can use the free online tools and resources developed especially for *In Focus* to learn additional unknown words from our NGSL and NAWL word lists.

All readings and written materials are graded to contain a very high percentage (90–95%) of high-frequency words from the NGSL. This helps develop students' reading fluency and confidence.

Though *In Focus* can be used as a standalone textbook, dedicated online elements enable students to personalize and extend their learning beyond the classroom. Among the online components are interactive flashcards, interactive dictionaries that show the keywords being used in authentic video clips, crossword and word search puzzles, speed reading exercises, supplemental graded readings for each unit, vocabulary worksheets, and audio recordings of all reading texts.

In Focus 1 is designed for students at a pre-intermediate level. Each unit is designed to help your students build both their knowledge as well as their ability to think critically about a wide range of important topics. The topics covered are advertising, sports, population changes and life extension, robots, how people use animals, and the internet and news. Language prompts are provided throughout to help students express themselves.

The *In Focus* Teacher's Manual contains full step-by-step teaching notes, unit-by-unit summaries, language notes, tips, extension activities, options for assessment, and a complete answer key.

We hope you and your students enjoy using *In Focus*.

Charles Browne

Brent Culligan

Joseph Phillips

How a unit works

All units in *In Focus* are eight pages long and follow a similar format. An audio icon reminds students they have the option of listening to the reading texts (available free from the website).

Unit organization

	Objective	Section
Page 1	Warm up Schema building Real-world connections	1 **Critical cartoons** Warm up Media link
Pages 2–3	Vocabulary development Reading Speaking	2 **Core vocabulary** Skimming and scanning Words in context: identifying a part of speech; word friends Word parts Discussion dictation
Pages 4–5	Reading Reading skills Speaking	3 **Reading skills** Pre-reading Reading Identifying topic and main idea Identifying unnecessary information; Logical reasoning; Finding supporting ideas Identifying opinions; Making inferences Discuss it
Page 6	Gathering, comparing, and analyzing information Speaking	4 **Find out more** Information gathering Comparing results
Pages 7–8	Critical thinking skills Writing Discussion	5 **Critical thinking** What does the author mean? Categorizing; Finding reasons and ranking them; Ranking Post your opinion Discussion Quotable Quotes

Unit sections

1 Critical cartoons

This is a short speaking activity centered on a cartoon related to the topic of the unit. All cartoons are authentic cartoons, and each was carefully chosen to represent the unit topic. Questions help activate schema and develop critical thinking skills.

2 Core vocabulary

Each unit teaches 10 important words from the New General Service List (NGSL). The section begins with a short reading passage (approximately 200 words) on an aspect of the unit topic that contextualizes the 10 keywords. A series of learning activities focuses on developing knowledge of collocations and analyzing and understanding word parts. This gives students practice using the words introduced in the unit. It also develops vocabulary learning skills and strategies that will be useful when encountering new words not introduced in the unit. A speaking activity rounds off this section.

3 Reading skills

Students work with a longer text (approximately 400 words) that gives a different or expanded point of view on the topic of the unit. This exposure to multiple points of view is a key aspect of developing skills in critical thinking. All 10 keywords appear in the second reading as well, providing additional in-context information about how the words are used. This is followed by a series of carefully structured activities including pre-reading, identifying the topic and main idea, finding supporting details, and logical reasoning. The section ends with a short discussion.

4 Find out more

Since information from various points of view is crucial to thinking critically about an issue, the pair or group activities in this section encourage students to gather further information related to the topic. This is followed by comparison and discussion of the information collected.

5 Critical thinking

Through pair, group, and open class work, students are encouraged to develop critical thinking skills, such as making inferences and ranking and categorizing data. Students then complete a writing task to express their opinion on the topic. The final page brings the content of the unit together in a discussion about the topic. Useful language prompts help students in each unit.

6 Quotable quotes

This final section introduces a quote by a famous person on the topic of the unit. Several thought-provoking questions on the quote conclude the unit. This section can be done in class as a short discussion activity or as a writing assignment outside the class.

To the student

Welcome to *In Focus*, a multi-level course for high school and university students. We have designed this series to help you build your vocabulary, work on all four basic skills (reading, writing, speaking, and listening), and help improve your discussion and presentation skills. *In Focus* will also help you think critically, which is a very important general academic skill. In each Student Book you will find 12 topic-based units. In addition to the Student Book, there is a range of free online components, which will help you focus on what you really need, learn more quickly, and become a more independent learner.

For *In Focus*, we have created a unique vocabulary syllabus containing the most important vocabulary words for learners of English. This list has a total of about 2,800 words, which are nearly all the words you will ever need. If you know these words, you will understand 92 percent of the words in most texts of general English (not bad, if you think that English has over 600,000 words!). You will learn 120 of these words in each book, 10 per unit. You can use the website and online tools developed especially for *In Focus* to learn the rest of the 2,800 words efficiently and enjoyably. Online, you will find a range of activities such as vocabulary puzzles, games, flashcards, and audio recordings of the reading texts.

In Focus 1 is designed for students at a pre-intermediate level. Each unit will help you build your knowledge about a wide range of interesting topics as well as help you think critically about these topics. You will learn about advertising, sports, population changes and living longer, robots, how people use animals, and the internet and news. In every unit, we also provide you with useful language and expressions where needed to help express yourself better.

We wish you good luck using *In Focus*. We are sure that the book and the online materials will help you to learn English quickly and in a fun way!

Charles Browne   Brent Culligan   Joseph Phillips

The World of Advertising

"You too? You didn't need it, you didn't want it, you didn't even know what it was, but you bought two."

In this unit, you will:

- read an article about advertising and brands.
- read an article about the negative effects of advertising.
- discuss some popular advertising techniques.

1 Critical cartoons

A Warm up

Work with a partner or in a small group. Look at the information on this page and the cartoon. Discuss the questions below.

1 How much advertising do you see in a typical day?

2 What kind of ads do you see most?

3 How do the ads make you feel?

4 What is the message of the cartoon? What is the connection to the unit topic?

> I see a lot of ads on ...

> The ads make me feel ...

> The ads I see are often about ...

> I think the ad is about ...

MEDIA link

The Greatest Movie Ever Sold (2011) is a funny documentary that asks the question, "Is it possible to fund a movie using only the money you get from advertising and product placements?" It is directed by Morgan Spurlock, creator of the hit documentary *Super Size Me*.

For additional media links, go to www.infocus-eltseries.com

2 Core vocabulary

A Skimming and scanning

1 Find and underline the keywords in the text. The first one is done for you. Then work with a partner, look at the text, and try to guess the meanings of the keywords.

Keywords

assume	behavior	brand	income	industry
label	prevent	stock	trend	warn

Advertising and Consumerism

Advertising is used in many ways. Health experts use advertising to warn the public against bad things. For example, they want to prevent young people from starting to smoke. They <u>assume</u> that young people 5 won't start if they know how bad smoking is. Sometimes, health organizations want to change people's behavior—getting them to exercise more, for example.

However, advertising is more often used by 10 industry to sell things. A company's income depends on how much money it makes by selling its products and services. These days, the trend is for companies to advertise their brand. A brand is a mark, a name, or 15 a label that stands for a company's products or services. In the past, a clothing company would advertise a coat or clothing.

Nowadays, a company might advertise how people feel when they wear its label. In this way, the company develops "brand loyalty." That is when people like to buy only the products 20 from one brand. Companies with brand loyalty can charge more money for their products. Investors in companies like brand loyalty very much because the price of their stock goes up when a company has a strong brand.

2 Read the statements below. Which best describes what this text is about? Circle A, B, or C. Then explain your answer to a partner.

A The uses of advertising in society

B The positive effects of brand loyalty

C How advertising can be used to improve our health

B Words in context: identifying a part of speech

1 Look at the text on page 2. Three of the keywords are verbs. Verbs describe an action. Find the verbs and write them below.

1 _____

2 _____

3 _____

2 The subject of the sentences is the same for all three verbs. Write it below.

_____

3 Use the three verbs to make your own sentences.

1 _____

2 _____

3 _____

C Word parts: *ism*   Example: *consumerism*

1 Find five words with *ism* in the puzzle and circle them. Check their meanings. See page 97 if you need help.

2 Complete the sentences below with the words from the puzzle.

1 There have been many acts of _____ _____ in the twenty-first century.

2 _____ is a belief that there is no god.

3 Many universities offer courses in _____.

4 Advertising encourages _____ in society.

5 _____ in Eastern Europe ended in the 1990s.

D	T	U	W	D	G	R	Z	U	S	W
C	O	N	S	U	M	E	R	I	S	M
C	B	S	N	F	I	U	M	S	S	V
O	N	A	V	O	B	S	F	I	X	F
M	Z	L	N	H	I	P	R	I	D	N
M	L	L	E	E	M	O	F	Y	J	J
U	T	Y	H	O	R	B	U	I	Y	H
N	J	T	V	R	V	K	A	U	R	C
I	A	G	E	E	J	X	M	M	K	A
S	Z	T	R	M	F	P	X	O	K	X
M	E	N	F	E	M	I	N	I	S	M

3 Work with a partner. What do you think *ism* means? Circle the correct answer.

A an outdoor activity

B a belief or system of beliefs

C thinking too much about something

D Discussion dictation

1 Listen and write down the questions.

1 What were _____ ?

2 What are _____ ?

3 Are cigarettes _____ ?

2 Work with a partner. Ask each other the questions. Be sure to ask follow-up questions.

3 Reading skills

A Pre-reading

1 Quickly scan the text and circle the 10 keywords.

2 Have you ever bought a product because of an advertisement you saw? What was it? Why did you buy it?

3 What is one positive effect and one negative effect of advertising?

B Reading

Read the text. Highlight an interesting idea in each paragraph.

You Are What You Buy

Over the last 70-80 years, consumerism has been a trend in many countries. People buy things they don't need, and they replace things before they wear out. [1] We used to repair things when they were broken, but today we throw out old things and replace them with new models. Indeed, many of the things we use can't be repaired. Once, products were made to last for many years. Now, they are
5   designed to last only a few years.

Advertising supports this behavior of buying things that we don't really need. Advertisements, or ads, make us notice products and brands because we see them frequently in our lives, especially on television. [2] There are many interesting programs on television. The advertising industry tells us that to be happy, we need their products in our lives. It does this with images that connect the product to happy,
10   successful, or beautiful people. We assume that to be successful or happy, we must buy the product or brand, or we must wear the same designer label as the beautiful, successful people in the ads.

The negative results of this consumerism are easy to see. [3] As people spend more and more of their income on things they don't need, they have to work more to pay for them. This prevents people from spending time with their families or spending money on education or healthy food. In America today,
15   there are four times more shopping centers than high schools. Many American parents say that they don't spend enough time with their children.

Another negative result is that we may believe things that aren't true. To increase profits and stock prices, companies make many false claims about their products. For example, can we really lose weight simply by
20   taking a pill, without dieting or exercising?

People also warn us of the negative effects of consumerism on the environment. [4] We use energy to produce these unnecessary goods, and that puts more carbon dioxide into the air, which causes climate change. When we throw away goods, they are either burned or buried,
25   again causing damage to the environment.

Advertisers say that all they do is inform us. But in reality, they have tricked us into working longer hours, buying stuff we don't need, and thinking we need their products to impress others.

C Identifying topic and main idea

Read the questions below and circle the correct answers according to the text.

1 Which of the following best describes the topic of the text?

   A Shopping

   B Consumerism

   C Fashion brands

   D Money

2 Which of the following best describes the main idea of the text?

   A Buying fashionable goods affects how people feel.

   B Modern products are not designed to last.

   C Advertising influences people's behavior in negative ways.

   D Consumerism has effects on the environment.

D Identifying unnecessary information

1 Look at the four numbered sentences in the passage. Which has information that is not related to the main point of the author?

Sentence number: _____

Reason it is not necessary: _____

2 Compare your answers with a partner.

E Identifying opinions

Which one of the following sentences best describes the author's opinion? Circle A, B, or C.

   A Advertising causes us to buy too many things, and this has many negative results.

   B Advertising is neither good nor bad; people can choose not to buy things.

   C Advertising is a useful way to find out about a product.

Work with a partner or in a small group. Ask and answer the questions below.

1 Look back at the ideas you highlighted. Are they the same? What are the differences?

2 You have 3 minutes. How many different types of advertising can you think of? For example, TV ads.

3 Imagine you want to buy these items: a mobile phone; a pair of shoes; a pizza. How important is advertising to you when you decide to buy these things?

A Information gathering

Work in small groups. Find at least five advertisements. If you can, go online to search for popular advertisements. Write notes about each one in the table below.

Advertisment	Product	Target Group	Why the ad appeals to target group
Photo of Shohei Ohtani	Oakley	Young people	Shohei Ohtani is young and successful

B Comparing results

Form new groups and compare your advertisements. Discuss the questions below.

1 How many of these products do you buy? How do you feel about them?

2 What words can you think of to describe the products?

3 Do the makers of any of these products use celebrities to advertise? If so, which? Does this make you want to buy the product?

4 Do any of the products use humor to sell the product? Which ones? Does this make you feel more positive about the product?

I think the advertisement for ... is original/funny/memorable/romantic.

The ad suggests / appeals to / features ...

Some / A lot of ads use celebrities. An example is ..., which uses ...

I like the way some advertisements ...

5 Critical thinking

A What does the author mean?

inference (n): a guess that something is true or not from the information you have

1 Work with a partner. Read the statements below and decide if they are suggested by the text on **page 4**. Write down your reasons.

Statement	Inference? (Yes/No)	Where (line no.)
1 In the past, products were of a higher quality.		
2 Consumerism causes parents to spend less time with their children.		
3 Advertisements are a reliable source of information.		
4 Advertising makes people assume they will be happy if they buy something.		

2 Compare your answers with a new partner.

B Categorizing

Read the statements below about some of the effects of advertising. Decide if they are positive or negative. Check (✓) the boxes. Then compare your answers with a partner.

Advertising . . .	Positive	Negative
creates more waste.	☐	☐
means people have to work harder.	☐	☐
increases company profits.	☐	☐
leads to less time with family.	☐	☐
gives more information to customers.	☐	☐
changes bad behavior.	☐	☐

C Post your opinion

1 Work with a partner or in a small group. Below are some common advertising techniques. Explain what you know about each technique.

1 Comparing products
2 Using creativity
3 Recommendation by a famous person
4 Using fear
5 Selling top-quality products at a high price
6 Focusing on lifestyle
7 Selling at a low price
8 Using scientific research

post (n, v): (to put) a message using social media

2 Which techniques are popular in your country? Which do you think are most effective? Write a post with your opinion.

> Here, one popular technique is ...

> I think the most effective technique is ...

D Discussion

1 Work in a small group. In C, you looked at eight advertising techniques. Read these statements taken from advertisements. Which techniques do they use? Write 1 to 8 in the table below

Advertising Statement	Technique (1–8)
TESTS SHOWED A 69% IMPROVEMENT AFTER USING BRAND A.	
Mouthwash A is better than Mouthwash B.	
Lionel Messi loves to use Brand C.	
30% off Brand X this week!	
Smoking shortens your life by 10 years.	
Enjoy life. Drive an XYZ and feel free.	

2 Another advertising technique is called "greenwashing." This is when a company says its products or activities are better for the environment than they really are. Look at the advertisement below and discuss the questions in your groups.

1 What is this ad for?

2 Do you think the ad is effective? Does it make you more likely to buy the product? What things does the ad NOT say about this product?

3 Why could this be an example of greenwashing?

4 Can you think of any other examples of greenwashing?

Fresh from the mountains
Mountain Top
Water

- All natural
- No calories
- No sugar
- 100% pure and healthy

Mountain Top
WATER

> Although the ad is probably telling the truth, I think …

> The ad doesn't say anything about …

> This could be an example of greenwashing because …

> Another example of greenwashing is …

Quotable quotes
Final thoughts . . .

Advertising is legalized* lying.

H. G. Wells
English writer

1 Do you think that ads sometimes lie? Give examples.

2 Do you think there should be laws on what and how products are advertised? Give examples.

*legalize (v): to allow by law

In this unit, you will:

- read an article about the pros and cons of advertising.
- read an article about how advertisers use the internet.
- design an ad for a product.

1 Critical cartoons

A Warm up

Work with a partner or in a small group. Look at the information on this page and the cartoon. Discuss the questions below.

1 What kind of things do you buy online?

2 After searching for something online, how often do you get suggestions to buy similar items? Give an example.

3 What is something you bought because you saw an ad for it?

4 What is the message of the cartoon? What is the connection to the unit topic?

> I always buy ... online.

> I saw an ad for ... I decided to ...

> I got a suggestion to buy ...

> I think the message of the ad is ...

MEDIA link

You're Soaking in It (2017) is a documentary that looks at the world of advertising. It shows how marketing companies collect people's data and target them with online ads.

For additional media links, go to www.infocus-eltseries.com

2 Core vocabulary

A Skimming and scanning

1 Find and underline the keywords in the text. The first one is done for you. Then work with a partner, look at the text, and try to guess the meanings of the keywords.

Keywords

award	benefit	blame	campaign	factor
mass	opportunity	promote	resource	technique

Advertising Techniques

It doesn't help to blame advertising for many of the world's problems. It is more useful to understand the techniques used to change people's behavior. Advertising researchers study people's reactions to different messages. The researchers look for factors that cause people to act in a certain way. For example, in a study of how children got their parents to buy them things, researchers watched children fight with their parents. This was an opportunity to learn how to make advertising more successful.

5

Some techniques are used to bring messages to a group. An example of this is the suggestions we see online that promote books similar to ones we have already bought. Other techniques bring messages to the mass of the population. For many years, Mothers Against Drunk Driving (MADD) organized a big campaign in North America. Their aim was to prevent people from drinking and driving. They used print and television ads to get their message across. As a result, drunk driving dropped in many American states. Some of these ads were so good they won <u>awards</u>.

10

15

20

Advertising is a communication resource. It can be put to good use to benefit society or used to bring harm or hurt. It just depends on the people using it.

2 Read the statements below. Which best summarizes the text? Circle A, B, or C. Then explain your answer to a partner.

A Advertising is neither good nor bad; it's just a form of communication.

B Advertising aimed at children persuades parents to buy certain products.

C Advertising stopped mothers from drunk driving.

B Words in context: word friends

1 Work with a partner. Look at the keywords below and the words that go with them. In each case, circle the one word that doesn't go with the keyword.

Keyword		Word friends			
1 (to) award _____	**A** a medal	**B** a trophy	**C** a prize	**D** a contest
2 _____ campaign	**A** high	**B** election	**C** national	**D** advertising
3 _____ technique	**A** research	**B** happy	**C** sales	**D** basic

2 Work with your partner. Choose one keyword plus one word friend and make your own sentence. Then read your sentence to another pair of students. Listen and write down their sentence.

Your sentence: _____

Other pair's sentence: _____

C Word parts: *con/com*   Example: *company*

1 Find five words with *con/com* in the puzzle and circle them. Check their meanings. See page 97 if you need help.

2 Complete the sentences below with the words from the puzzle.

1 Jerry works for a _____ that designs websites.

2 These days, cell phones are _____ and light.

3 If you _____ red and yellow, you get orange.

4 Using the internet on a cell phone is very _____.

5 The iPhone is a great example of _____ design.

G	N	E	T	M	J	T	I	N	G	W	C
X	C	O	M	B	I	N	E	R	N	P	O
P	E	O	W	M	H	F	Q	X	N	M	M
U	U	O	U	B	U	H	H	O	V	S	P
C	O	N	V	E	N	I	E	N	T	J	A
D	G	P	B	D	I	Q	U	X	V	K	N
C	O	N	T	E	M	P	O	R	A	R	Y
T	H	S	Z	Z	R	M	N	M	J	C	G
M	Y	P	U	O	K	M	X	P	U	O	Q
Z	W	H	W	U	C	G	P	L	A	O	M
S	D	Z	E	O	C	O	M	P	A	C	T
D	K	A	C	B	U	S	N	J	Q	C	F

3 Work with a partner. What do you think *con/com* means? Circle the correct answer.

A not

B together or with

C modern or new

D Discussion dictation

1 Listen and write down the questions.

1 Do you have _____?

2 What _____?

3 Are there _____?

2 Work with a partner. Ask each other the questions. Be sure to ask follow-up questions.

Reading skills

A Pre-reading

1 Quickly scan the text and circle the 10 keywords.

2 Do you sometimes receive email or messages from people you don't know? What are they about?

3 Email and browser providers sometimes search through your private information. Why do they do this?

B Reading

Read the text. Highlight an interesting idea in each paragraph.

How Advertisers Use the Internet

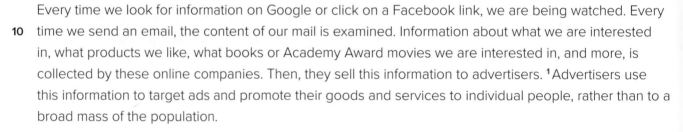

We have all become users of free online applications. Google, Yahoo, Facebook, and others provide convenient resources, such as email, messaging, and search tools. Millions of people use these sites every day. How do technology
5 companies benefit by supplying services for free? The answer is that although we assume that we are customers of Google or Facebook, in fact we are not. We are the product that these companies sell to their real customers: advertisers.

Every time we look for information on Google or click on a Facebook link, we are being watched. Every
10 time we send an email, the content of our mail is examined. Information about what we are interested in, what products we like, what books or Academy Award movies we are interested in, and more, is collected by these online companies. Then, they sell this information to advertisers. ¹Advertisers use this information to target ads and promote their goods and services to individual people, rather than to a broad mass of the population.

15 As technology improves, the opportunity for advertisers to target customers grows. Smartphones can show a person's location as well as a lot of other personal information. Online companies sell this information to advertisers. For example, imagine that your hobby is tennis. You have recently searched online for a new racket. You are walking down the street and suddenly you receive a message from a sports store, informing you of a sales campaign for tennis rackets. You look up and see the store right in
20 front of you. ²Practicing your technique is important if you want to improve in tennis.

Internet companies know our hobbies and interests, our likes and dislikes, and so much more. They even know about our children. More than a quarter of parents in the United States have posted photos of their children online. These include names and sometimes even addresses. Companies can collect all this information and sell it to advertisers. But do they have the right to do this? There are many factors
25 to think about. ³We can blame them for the junk email that we all receive. We can also blame them for the annoying pop-ups we see online. ⁴The companies say that they are just connecting buyers and sellers. They say that they are helping people to find the right products and services. However, these companies are using our personal information for their own profit.

C Identifying topic and main idea

Read the questions below and circle the correct answers according to the text.

1 Which of the following best describes the topic of the text?

    A Internet advertising

    B Free online resources

    C Google and Facebook

    D How stores sell their products

2 Which of the following best describes the main idea of the text?

    A As we use computers, companies look for information about our children.

    B As we use the internet, companies collect and sell information about us.

    C Google and Facebook's real customers are people, not advertisers.

    D We will probably have to pay to use internet sites in the future.

D Identifying unnecessary information

1 Look at the four numbered sentences in the text. Which contains information that is not related to the main point of the author?

Sentence number: _____

Reason it is not necessary: _____

2 Compare your answers with a partner.

E Identifying opinions

Which one of the following people agrees with the author?

Ben: Companies like Google should not be allowed to collect my private search history.

Rina: There's no need to worry about giving some private information on the internet. Companies need it.

Ann: I think the more Amazon knows about me, the better my shopping will be.

Work with a partner or in a small group. Ask and answer the questions below.

1 Look back at the ideas you highlighted. Are they the same? What are the differences?

2 Read what Sara did today. If companies have information about her day, what kind of products do you think they could try and sell her?

> "I read the news online. There was an interesting article about how to get fit. I googled Italian recipes for dinner tonight. I read an email from my son. He wants to visit next weekend with his girlfriend and talk about their wedding. He asked me to book a flight for him."

3 Think about a recent day when you used the internet. What kind of advertising might you receive?

4 Find out more

A Information gathering

1 Work with a partner. Advertisers use many techniques to sell their products. Below is a list of some common techniques. Read the list and check you understand the meaning of each technique. Check online if you need to.

Technique	This technique ...
Cause and effect	tells you that if you use this product or service, your problems will disappear.
Comparison	compares a product or service with the competition.
Fame appeal	links a product or service with a famous person.
Jargon	uses technical words to impress.
Label	links a product or service with a brand.
Price appeal	tells you that you are getting something extra for less money.
Sex appeal	tells you that the product will make you more attractive.
Slogan	links a product or service with an idea.
Testimonial	gets people, sometimes famous, to say they like the product.

2 Work in small groups. Think of different advertisements used to sell products on TV, online, in magazines and newspapers, or on the radio. Use the list above to help you decide which technique is used in each case. Write the advertisement and its technique in the table below.

Advertisement	Technique
Just Do It (Nike)	Slogan

B Comparing results

Discuss the questions below with the class.

1 How many different techniques did you find? Which is the most popular?

2 What techniques are used most in your country? Why? Are there any not on the list?

3 Which techniques do you like most? Which do you think work best? Why?

> Our group found that the most popular technique was ...

> A technique used in this country is ...

> We think the best technique is ... because ...

5 Critical thinking

A What does the author mean?

1 Work with a partner. Read the statements below and decide if they are suggested by the text on page 12. Write down your reasons.

Statement	Inference? (Yes/No)	Where (line no.)
1 Advertisers send us junk email.		
2 Internet companies read your personal email.		
3 New technology can save you money by telling you about special offers.		
4 Parents want companies to know about their children.		

2 Compare your answers with a new partner.

B Ranking

1 Many websites ask for personal information. What information are you happy to give? Rank the website types below. Write 1 to 3 in the columns (1 = no problem, happy to give; 2 = not happy, but necessary; 3 = not OK to give).

Website type	Personal information	Happy to give (1-3)		
		You	Group	Class
Online bookstore	Address			
	Income			
Online travel agent	Cell phone number			
	Hobbies/Interests			
Social media site	Address			
	Single? Married?			
Your bank	Income			
	Single? Married?			

2 Form small groups and compare your rankings. Write your group rankings in the table above.

> I would never allow ...

> Personally, I think it's OK to give ...

3 Compare your group ranking with other groups in the class. Write your class rankings in the table above.

> It's dangerous to ...

> I don't understand why people worry about ...

C Post your opinion

Read the statements below. Choose one. Write a short post with your opinion about it.

1 Internet advertising practices are not different from television ads. They are just better.

2 Without advertising, many people would have unhappier lives.

3 It's OK for people to get paid to write online product reviews.

D Discussion

Work in small groups. In C, you wrote about the issue of privacy, personal information, and online advertising. Now you are going to design an online advertisement. One person in the group should take notes.

1 First, think of a product or service. The list below may help you.

camera	energy drink	running shoes
car	English language school	smartphone
college	fashion brand	travel
computer or tablet	restaurant	watch

2 Now plan your online advertisement for the product or service. Look back at the advertising techniques on **page 14**. Choose one or two of these techniques to help you design your ad. Then think about:

- the people you are advertising to
- the main message
- the key information that you want to present
- an interesting image
- the design of the advertisement (size, color, font, etc.)
- the star or stars of the advertisement

3 Present your advertisement to the class. Students who are listening should ask follow-up questions.

Our advertisement is for ...

Our main message is ...

Did you think about ...?

The technique we decided to use is ...

Why did you decide to ...?

We decided to focus on ... because ...

How did you choose the ...?

Was it difficult to ...

4 Decide as a class which advertisement is the most effective. Discuss the good and bad points of each ad.

The advertisement for ... was really effective, because ...

I wouldn't buy ... because ...

Quotable quotes
Final thoughts ...

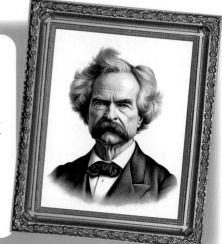

Many a small thing has been made large by the right kind of advertising.

Mark Twain
American writer

1 Why do you think people buy so many things they don't need?

2 What unimportant or small things have become popular because of advertising?

"Marcia, how many lives do I have left?"

In this unit, you will:

- read an article about extreme athletes.
- read an article about people who take extreme risks for pleasure.
- discuss who is responsible when extreme sports go wrong.

1 Critical cartoons

A Warm up

Work with a partner or in a small group. Look at the information on this page and the cartoon. Discuss the questions below.

1 "A cat has 9 lives" is a popular idiom in English. What do you think it means? Look it up online and check.

2 What "extreme" sports do you know? Why are they called extreme?

3 If you could try any extreme activity, what would it be? Why?

4 Why is the cat in the cartoon asking the question? What is the connection to the unit topic?

I think this idiom means ...

One extreme sport I know is ...

I would try ... because ...

I think the cat is asking because ...

MEDIA link

Free Solo (2018) is an Academy Award-winning documentary. It is about Alex Honnold's amazing attempt to climb El Capitan on his own, with no ropes or help. Many people think it is one of the great physical achievements in human history.

For additional media links, go to www.infocus-eltseries.com

A Skimming and scanning

1 Find and underline the keywords in the text. The first one is done for you. Try to guess their meanings.

Keywords

achieve	athlete	coach	complain	feature
further	seek	suggestion	typically	victim

Extreme Athletes

In 2011, Antoine Montant became yet another victim of an extreme sport.

He was killed while BASE jumping in France. BASE jumpers jump off high places with a wingsuit and a parachute.
5 Montant's parachute didn't open. It took search and rescue workers two days to find his body in the mountains.

Montant was a famous extreme athlete who lived in the mountains of France. Extreme athletes typically do sports that are more dangerous than regular sports. Montant
10 learned to ski from a very early age. He soon became an instructor and coach. When he was nine, he began paragliding. His love of excitement led him to seek ways to bring both sports together. He wanted to increase the excitement further. Montant made many suggestions
15 before he <u>achieved</u> his goal and invented "speed riding." This extreme sport has two of the features of his favorite sports: skis and parachutes. In speed riding, the athlete skis down a high mountain while wearing a small parachute.

20 Many people complain that life is boring. Extreme athletes like Montant want to enjoy life as much as possible. Montant was an athlete who died doing what he loved.

2 Read the titles below. Which would also be a good title for the text? Circle A, B, or C. Then explain your answer to a partner.

A The Dangers of Extreme Sports

B The Life and Death of Antoine Montant

C The Growing Sport of BASE Jumping

B Words in context: identifying a part of speech

1 Look at the text on page 18. Find the keywords that are used in the text. Which are verbs and which are adverbs? Write them below. Verbs describe an action, and adverbs describe verbs.

Verb	Adverb
1 _____	4 _____
2 _____	5 _____
3 _____	

2 Use the adverbs to write your own sentences.

1 _____

2 _____

C Word parts: *para*   Example: *parachute*

1 Put the sentences below in the right order to make a short story. Try to guess the meaning of any words you don't know.

_____ In the middle of writing a paragraph she stopped.

_____ A passenger saw the mountain and suddenly became paranoid.

_____ She put down her pen, grabbed a parachute, and jumped out of the plane.

_____ A small plane was flying parallel to a mountain.

_____ She was a paramedic writing about a patient.

2 Complete the sentences below with words from the story.

1 Erica works in a hospital as a _____.

2 Terry couldn't stop feeling _____, so his doctor gave him some medicine.

3 Samuel wrote a _____ about his summer vacation.

4 The highway ran _____ to the coast.

5 After the pilot jumped from the plane, her _____ opened safely.

3 Work with a partner. What do you think *para* means? Circle the correct answer.

A something that is similar to, beside, or protects against another thing

B something that is under or beneath another thing

C something that is part of or belonging to life

D Discussion dictation

1 Listen and write down the questions.

1 What is the _____ ?

2 What are some _____ ?

3 Why do you think _____ ?

2 Work with a partner. Ask each other the questions. Be sure to ask follow-up questions.

A Pre-reading

1 Quickly scan the text and circle the **10** keywords.

2 Compare the three activities shown in the photos below. How are they similar?

3 If you had to choose, which activity would you prefer to do? Which do you find the most frightening? Why?

B Reading

Read the text. Highlight an interesting idea in each paragraph.

Extreme Activities, Extreme Risks

It's not only athletes who choose excitement. Danger and adventure also attract many others to high-risk activities. But with the excitement comes the possibility of accidents and costly results.

5 Many sad events raise questions about extreme sports and high-risk activities. One was an accident in 2015 on Mount Everest. Another happened in 2023 and featured a deep-sea diving ship called Titan.

The Everest accident in 2015 was the worst in its history. An
10 earthquake caused a huge avalanche*. There were 19 victims. Fast-forward to 2023, and we saw the Titan disaster. During its journey to the bottom of the sea to see the wreck** of the Titanic, something went wrong, and a rescue attempt was begun. The rescue efforts faced several challenges, especially
15 the extreme depth of the Titanic. Dangerous weather conditions further added to the problem. All five passengers died. Events like these make us question why people do such dangerous activities.

People take part in many kinds of high-risk activities. As well as climbing Everest or deep-ocean diving, there is also wingsuit flying, parasailing, and BASE jumping, to name a few. What makes people do these activities? Typically, people seek excitement. They want to go beyond safe limits and feel happy when they achieve a challenging goal. Not all of these people are athletes with professional coaches. Sometimes, people with only basic skills try to do what seems impossible, like climbing the highest mountains. They sometimes pay a huge sum of money for this. For example, it costs up to $65,000 to climb Everest, as much as $250,000 to dive to the Titanic, and up to $55 million for a trip to space.

When people don't have the skills they need to achieve these very difficult things, accidents happen, like on Mount Everest or at the bottom of the sea. In many cases, the accidents result in emergency rescues. These rescues can be very expensive, and rescuers sometimes even lose their lives. So, people often complain. They ask who should pay: those taking part or society?

Some people have even made the suggestion that high-risk sports and activities should be against the law. They believe that would help society. However, others argue that this would take away personal freedoms and our ability to explore. Sadly, one thing is certain: there will be more accidents and deaths as people continue to seek excitement.

*avalanche (n): a situation when snow and ice fall down a mountain
**wreck (n): a ship that has been very badly damaged

C Identifying topic and main idea

Read the questions below and circle the correct answers according to the text.

1 Is the author's opinion about the topic of extreme activities positive, neutral, or negative?

2 Which of the following best describes the main idea of the text?

    A Extreme activities are very risky and place a cost on society.

    B Most extreme activities take place in and on the water.

    C Extreme activities should be banned because they are too expensive.

    D Extreme sports are dangerous but fun and exciting.

D Logical reasoning

1 Some people argue that extreme activities should be banned because they put the rescuers in danger. Which of the following statements would make this argument weaker?

    A Sixty percent of search and rescue workers do extreme activities.

    B The most useful rescue tools were made by people who do extreme activities.

    C Almost all rescue workers' injuries happen during normal rescues.

2 Compare your answers with a partner.

E Identifying opinions

Which two of these three opinions would the author probably agree with?

    A The deaths of the five people on the Titan was sad and unnecessary.

    B The 19 people who died on Everest in 2015 were heroes.

    C Many people participate in extreme activities without the skills they need.

Work with a partner or in a small group. Ask and answer the questions below.

1 Look back at the ideas you highlighted. Are they the same? What are the differences?

2 When accidents happen with extreme activities, the cost of rescue can also be extreme. Who do you think should pay?

4 Find out more

1 Work with a partner. Which verbs (*play, do,* or *go*) go with each sport in the table below? Write the verbs on the lines.

2 Put checks (✓) next to the sports you play and rank how dangerous you think they are (1 = not dangerous; 5 = very dangerous). Have you ever been injured while doing these sports? Write Yes or No.

3 Interview your partner and put checks (✓) next to the sports he or she plays.

play, do, or *go*	Sport	You	Dangerous? (1–5)	Injured? (Yes/No)	Your partner: _____
play	American football				
	baseball				
	cycling				
	hockey				
	karate				
	sailing				
	skiing				
	soccer				
	surfing				
	swimming				
	table tennis				

B Comparing results

Discuss the questions below as a class.

1 Which sports are the most popular in your class? Which are the least popular?

2 What is the most dangerous sport anyone in your class has tried?

3 Has anyone in the class ever been injured in a sport?

The most/least popular/dangerous sport in class is ...

Only a few classmates ...

We couldn't agree which sport is most/least ...

Most injuries in the class came from ...

5 Critical thinking

A What does the author mean?

1 Work with a partner. Read the statements below and decide if they are suggested by the text on page 20. Write down your reasons.

Statement	Inference? (Yes/No)	Where (line no.)
1 If you have enough money, you can go to the top of Mount Everest.		
2 People seeking excitement always use special equipment.		
3 Extreme activities are dangerous to the people who do them, and they are dangerous to other people as well.		

2 Compare your answers with a new partner.

B Finding reasons and ranking them

"I bike 15 kilometers and swim 1 kilometer daily. Why? I want to control my weight and live to an old age. And it makes me feel good." *Rachel (29), San Francisco*

1 Work in small groups. What three reasons does Rachel give for doing sports? What are other reasons for people doing sports or extreme sports? Make a list.

2 Work with your classmates. You have 5 minutes. Interview as many people as possible. Ask them why they do sports. Make notes in the table below.

Reasons why people do sports	Number of responses	Popularity

3 What are the most common reasons? Rank them in order of popularity.

C Post your opinion

In 2023, Jennie Chong broke both arms in a terrible bungee-jumping accident. A few months later, she was planning to jump again!

Imagine you are Jennie's best friend. It is just after the accident, and Jennie has told you she wants to bungee jump again. Send her a message with your opinion about her decision.

D Discussion

Simon always wanted to parasail. He went to parasailing school last week. On the second day of instruction, in a strong wind, he crashed and broke both legs. As a result, he has lost his job and must pay $15,000 in medical expenses.

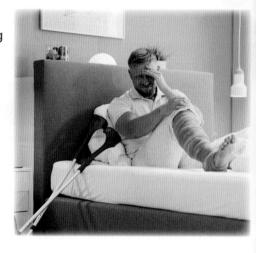

Simon is now talking to a lawyer about whether to claim against ...

- the parasailing school
- the parasailing teacher
- the parasail maker
- the weather forecaster (the forecast that day was light wind)

1 Work in small groups. Discuss the situation. Who should pay? Give your reasons and come to an agreement.

Looking at all the facts, ...

In this case, I think that ...

Well, it's difficult to say, because ...

It's clear to me that ... should pay because ...

2 Explain your choice and reasons to another group or to the class.

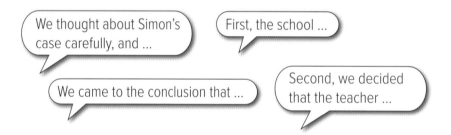

We thought about Simon's case carefully, and ...

First, the school ...

We came to the conclusion that ...

Second, we decided that the teacher ...

Quotable quotes
Final thoughts . . .

I want to stay as close to the edge as I can without going over. Out on the edge you see all kinds of things you can't see from the center.

Kurt Vonnegut
American writer

1 How is this quote connected to the topic of this unit?

2 Vonnegut talks about "going over." What do you think he means?

3 "Life on the edge" means living life doing exciting or dangerous activities. Do you know anyone who lives life on the edge? What do they do?

In this unit, you will:

- read an article about competition and winning.
- read an article about drugs in sports.
- discuss competition in the real world.

1 Critical cartoons

A Warm up

Work with a partner or in a small group. Look at the information on this page and the cartoon. Discuss the questions below.

1 Do you know any famous athletes who cheated? What do you know about them?

2 What are steroids? Why do people take them? Check online.

3 What are some reasons people cheat?

4 What is the message of the cartoon? What is the connection to the unit topic?

> One athlete I know is …

> One reason people cheat is …

> I think people take steroids because …

> I think the connection to the unit topic is …

MEDIA link

Bad Sport (2021) is a Netflix true-crime series that focuses on some of the biggest issues in sports. Each episode focuses on one problem and is about a different sport.

For additional media links, go to www.infocus-eltseries.com

A Skimming and scanning

1 Find and underline the keywords in the text. The first one is done for you. Try to guess their meanings.

Keywords

bill	competition	deliver	increase	mention
observe	plus	rate	root	status

How to Do Better

Life often seems to be a competition to see who is faster, stronger, or smarter. Winning is very important because it affects our status and income. Athletes can get big increases in their incomes when they win. In school, students compete for grades and awards. At work, employees compete for promotions. They must help their companies deliver new and better products and services if they want to achieve success. All of this comes at a cost, and the <u>bill</u>   5
is usually paid for in time, effort, and health. Great effort plus the fear of falling behind can make people sick, and it is the root of many illnesses in modern society.

As mentioned, winning is important, so people always look for ways to improve their chances. Sometimes, it is possible to win by more training, studying, or eating better. But another option is to take drugs that will improve performance. Some athletes take drugs to   10

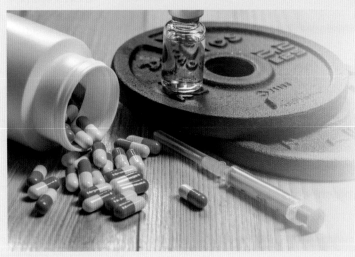

increase their heart rates, while some students and employees take drugs to increase their concentration. Many of these drugs are allowed but are not used in the   15
correct way. Police have observed that more and more of these drugs are sold on the streets or over the internet. This trend will probably continue because they give people   20
the chance to do more and perform better than others.

2 Read the titles below. Which would also be a good title for the text? Circle A, B, or C. Then explain your answer to a partner.

A Similarities Between Students and Athletes

B Winning Is Everything

C The Root of Illness

B Words in context: word friends

1 Work with a partner. Look at the keywords below and the words that go with them. In each case, circle the one word that doesn't go with the keyword.

Keyword	Word friends			
1 (to) observe _____	**A** behavior	**B** trends	**C** bills	**D** people
2 _____ rate	**A** monthly	**B** average	**C** growth	**D** thick
3 _____ increase	**A** long	**B** possible	**C** sharp	**D** large

2 Work with your partner. Choose one keyword plus one word friend and make your own sentence. Then read your sentence to another pair of students. Listen and write down their sentence.

Your sentence: _____

Other pair's sentence: _____

C Word parts: *port* Example: *export*

1 Put the sentences below in the right order to make a short story. Try to guess the meaning of any words you don't know.

_____ As a result, the person was deported.

_____ Her job was to check every import and export.

_____ Jenny started working at a busy airport.

_____ Jenny ended her day by writing a report about the event.

_____ One day, she caught someone trying to export something against the law.

2 Complete the sentences below with words from the story.

1 The _____ of tropical fruits added new flavors to the local market.

2 The weather _____ predicts heavy rainfall tomorrow.

3 The government will _____ anyone who has entered the country in the wrong way.

4 She arrived at the _____ two hours before her flight.

5 Hawaii's largest fruit _____ is pineapples.

3 Work with a partner. What do you think *port* means? Circle the correct answer.

A to travel

B to carry

C to give

D Discussion dictation

1 Listen and write down the questions.

1 Have you ever _____?

2 What kinds of ___ _____?

3 How important is _____?

2 Work with a partner. Ask each other the questions. Be sure to ask follow-up questions.

3 Reading skills

1 Quickly scan the text and circle the 10 keywords.

2 What are some of the ways people cheat in sports?

3 What advantages do rich athletes have compared with poorer ones? Think of at least two.

B Reading

Read the text. Highlight an interesting idea in each paragraph.

Drugs in Sport

Competition is a natural feature of life. In fact, it is the root of success. Competition at high school leads to better grades and the chance to go to a good university. Winning in business leads to a
5 better career, higher status, and higher income. Without competition, people become lazy. They don't do what they should and refuse to work hard.

Competition is most obvious in sports. Competition in sports is hard. Athletes must train for hours
10 every day. Sometimes, they seek other ways to increase their performance and use drugs and other chemical substances. As the rate of drug use increases, sports organizations try to prevent their use. They do this by testing the athletes' blood. If they find signs of drug use, they can ban athletes from future events. Sports organizations explain that
15 they have to do this for two reasons. First, they say that drugs deliver an unfair advantage. Second, they mention that the use of drugs is bad for athletes' health.

The first argument really makes no sense to me. Ideally, the rules athletes observe should be the same. But they never are. Rich athletes can pay the bill for expensive training equipment and special coaches. They can buy high-tech shoes and clothing that give them an advantage. Plus, athletes from developed
20 countries often have sponsors, so they don't need to work and train at the same time. In addition, rich athletes may be able to pay for new drugs that aren't banned.

The argument that banning drugs protects athletes is difficult to believe. Athletes are usually tested after an event. If banned substances are discovered, they are fined and lose their status. They can't compete for a period of time. These punishments have become more and more strict, but drug use in sports has
25 gone up, not down. The present system doesn't result in fewer athletes using drugs. Instead, athletes look for substances that tests can't find. These substances are often more dangerous than banned substances.

So, if banning drugs doesn't increase fairness or protect athletes' health, what should we do? The best answer is to control their use. They should be available to athletes under a doctor's care. All athletes
30 should have the same chance to use them, and a doctor can help protect their health. Instead of banning these substances, we should accept reality and control them.

C Identifying topic and main idea

Read the questions below and circle the correct answers according to the text.

1   Which of the following best describes the topic of the text?

   A   Sports and drugs

   B   Breaking records

   C   The danger of drugs

   D   Banning dangerous sports

2   Which of the following best describes the main idea of the text?

   A   Athletes should be tested for drug use on a daily basis.

   B   Athletes should be allowed to cheat.

   C   We should control rather than ban drug use in sports.

   D   Punishing athletes for drug use is the best way to prevent drug use in sports.

D Logical reasoning

1   The author argues that athletes should be able to use drugs. Which of the following would support this view?

   A   Medicines that help athletes get better quickly help thousands of ordinary people.

   B   Many athletes can't take common medicines because of drug bans. This puts the athletes' health at risk.

   C   Many advanced technologies, such as jet engines and nuclear energy, are the result of the most extreme type of competition: war.

2   Compare your answers with a partner.

E Identifying opinions

Which one of the following people agrees with the author?

Naomi: Athletes who use drugs are cheats and should not be allowed to compete.

Jason: That's right. Punishing athletes who cheated reduced the number of drug users at the last Olympics.

Maria: I think we need to control drug use. I'm not sure banning drugs is the answer.

Discuss it

Work with a partner or in a small group. Ask and answer the questions below.

1   Look back at the ideas you highlighted. Are they the same? What are the differences?

2   Have you or has someone you know done any of these things?

   •   Cheated in a game of cards

   •   Copied and pasted from the internet when doing your homework

   •   Pretended to work overtime

   •   Put false information on your résumé

   •   Ridden on a bus or train without paying

3   Discuss how bad you think each of these things is. What should the punishment be for each of them?

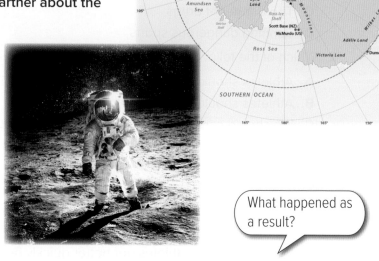

4 Find out more

A Information gathering

Work with a partner. One is Student A; one is Student B.
Four cases of competition in the real world are listed below.
Student A: look at **page 97**; Student B: look at **page 101**.
Take turns asking and answering your partner about the
missing information. Fill in the table.

Real-world competition

1 Apple v. Google

2 Lewis Hamilton v. Nico Rosberg

3 Scott v. Amundsen

4 USSR v. USA space race

> What was the situation between ...?

> What happened as a result?

B Comparing results

1 Work in small groups. Think of two more real examples of competition. Write in the table.

Competition	Situation	Result

2 Describe your examples to the class. Discuss whether the results in each case were positive, negative, or both.

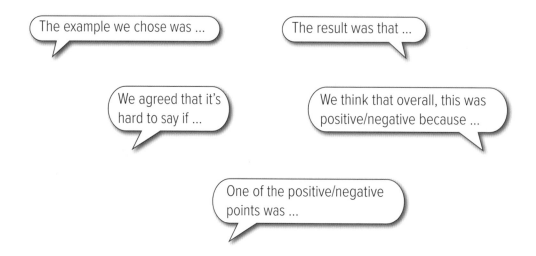

> The example we chose was ...

> The result was that ...

> We agreed that it's hard to say if ...

> We think that overall, this was positive/negative because ...

> One of the positive/negative points was ...

5 Critical thinking

A What does the author mean?

1 Work with a partner. Read the statements below and decide if they are suggested by the text on page 28. Write down your reasons.

Statement	Inference? (Yes/No)	Where (line no.)
1 Competition encourages people to do their best.		
2 Athletes in developing countries use drugs more.		
3 Sports organizations encourage safety.		
4 The best solution is to ban all drugs in sports.		

2 Compare your answers with a new partner.

B Ranking

In which sports and activities are people likely to use drugs to improve performance? Rank the activities below from 1 to 5 (1 = least likely; 5 = most likely). Then compare your answers with a partner.

100-meter sprint	_____	sailing	_____
a long overnight drive	_____	studying for an exam	_____
baseball	_____	watching a late-night movie	_____
bowling	_____	weightlifting	_____
driving to work	_____		

C Post your opinion

1 The text on page 28 suggests that athletes should be able to choose if they want to use drugs. Should the activities listed below also be a matter of personal choice? Discuss them with a partner.

Activity	Should be controlled? (Yes/No)
1 Riding a motorcycle without a helmet	
2 Riding a bicycle without a helmet	
3 Eating high-fat or high-sugar food	
4 Smoking tobacco	
5 Using e-cigarettes	

2 Choose one of the activities and write a post with your opinion.

D Discussion

1 Work in small groups. Look at the diagram below. It shows different types of competition. Think of as many examples as you can for each type. Add them to the diagram.

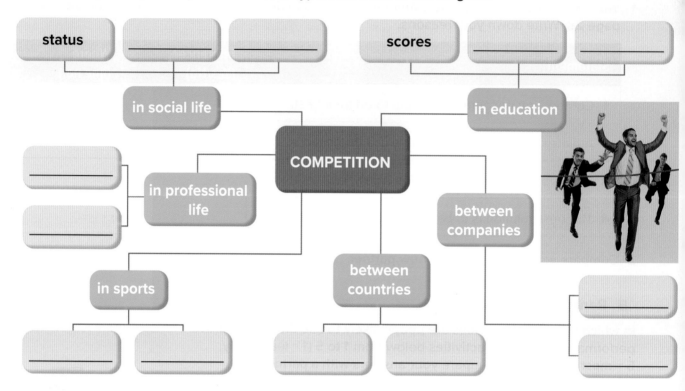

status ___ ___

scores ___ ___

in social life

in education

COMPETITION

___ ___

in professional life

between companies

in sports

between countries

___ ___

___ ___

___ ___

___

2 What do people, companies, and countries do to compete? Give examples. Which do you think are fair and which are unfair? Discuss with your partners.

> One type of competition I think is fair is ...

> Some people/countries will do anything to ...

> There are several ways people can get to the top. For example, ...

> I don't think ... is right because ...

3 Share your ideas with the class. Students who are listening should ask follow-up questions.

Quotable quotes
Final thoughts . . .

If you aren't going all the way, why go at all?

Joe Namath
American football player

Winning isn't everything. It's the only thing.

Vince Lombardi
American football coach

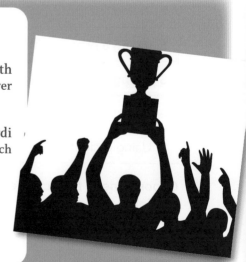

1 Explain the quotes in your own words. What do they have in common?

2 What is the connection between the quotes and athletes who take banned drugs?

"We're launching a campaign to get people to take up smoking again!"

In this unit, you will:
- read an article about aging populations.
- read an article about problems and solutions to low birthrates.
- discuss issues affecting the elderly.

1 Critical cartoons

A Warm up

Work with a partner or in a small group. Look at the information on this page and the cartoon. Discuss the questions below.

> In my country, there are more and more ...

1 What is a "time bomb"? Check online.

2 How is the population in your country changing? How about the number of elderly people?

> One problem is ...

> The percentage of ... is increasing.

3 Does this cause your country any problems? Give an example.

> I think the idea of the cartoon is ...

4 What is the idea of the cartoon? What is the connection to the unit topic?

MEDIA link

Plan 75 (2022) is a film by Chie Hayakawa. It is about a plan to pay people over 75 to kill themselves, to control Japan's aging population. The film is more like a documentary than a movie.

For additional media links, go to www.infocus-eltseries.com

A Skimming and scanning

1 Find and underline the keywords in the text. The first one is done for you. Try to guess their meanings.

Keywords

average	category	duty	growth	ignore
material	option	separate	solution	supply

Time to Relax?

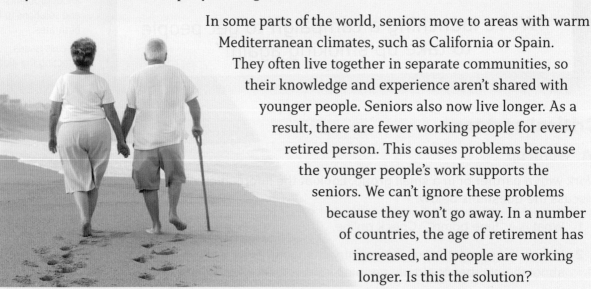

One way to understand the future of a society is to look at the age of its population. When the number of people gets bigger over time, this is population growth. If we add up the ages of all people in a country and divide it by the total number of people, we get the <u>average</u> age of the population. In many countries, this average age is increasing. The biggest growth is taking place in the category known as "seniors," people over 60 or 65. Many of them   5
have worked hard for most of their lives. They worked to supply society with the services it needed or in industries that made important materials. They feel that they have done their duty to society. After they stop working, most of them have the option to receive money every month from their company or the government.

In some parts of the world, seniors move to areas with warm   10
Mediterranean climates, such as California or Spain.
They often live together in separate communities, so
their knowledge and experience aren't shared with
younger people. Seniors also now live longer. As a
result, there are fewer working people for every   15
retired person. This causes problems because
the younger people's work supports the
seniors. We can't ignore these problems
because they won't go away. In a number
of countries, the age of retirement has   20
increased, and people are working
longer. Is this the solution?

2 Which picture goes best with the text? Circle A, B, or C. Then explain your answer to a partner.

A

B

C

B Words in context: identifying a part of speech

1 Look at the text on page 34. Two of the keywords are adjectives. Adjectives describe a noun. Find them and the nouns that go with them. Write them below.

Adjective	Noun
1 _____	_____
2 _____	_____

2 Use the adjectives to write your own sentences.

1 _____

2 _____

C Word parts: *medi*   Example: *Mediterranean*

1 Using the clues below, find words with *medi* and do the crossword puzzle. See page 98 or use a dictionary if you need help.

Across

2 The middle number or amount in a series

3 Not high quality

4 Period in the past from about 500 to 1500 CE

Down

1 The sea that has southern Europe, North Africa, and the Middle East around it

2 To try to solve a disagreement between people by talking to them

2 Complete the sentences below with the words from the puzzle. Change the word form as necessary.

1 The _____ family income in Canada is about 70,000 Canadian dollars.

2 Leona's grades in math were _____, but she did well in history.

3 Tina tried to _____ between the two arguing families.

4 Italy and Spain are _____ countries.

5 King John was a _____ ruler of England.

3 Work with a partner. What do you think *medi* means? Circle the correct answer.

A not big or small

B related to a drug given by a doctor

C something that is between two other things

D Discussion dictation

1 Listen and write down the questions.

1 Where would you _____?

2 What kind of _____?

3 Do you think _____?

2 Work with a partner. Ask each other the questions. Be sure to ask follow-up questions.

3 Reading skills

A Pre-reading

1 Quickly scan the text and circle the 10 keywords.

2 The average length of life is called life expectancy. Try to match the countries and life expectancy. Then check your answers on **page 98**.

Country	Life expectancy
Argentina Ethiopia Germany	79 65 73 85
Japan Russia South Africa USA	68 77 82

3 Why do you think life expectancy varies from country to country?

B Reading

Read the text. Highlight an interesting idea in each paragraph.

Growing Old

If we could travel back in time 150 years or so, what would we notice as we stepped out of our time machine? Of course, there would be no electronic devices or things made out of plastic. There would be no radio, no TV, and no planes in the sky. However, perhaps the biggest change from the world we know would be the large number of children that we would see. Since that time, especially in developed
5   countries, the average age of people has increased all over the world. In developed countries, the median age of a country's population—the age at which there are the same numbers of older and younger people—was 29 in 1950 and 37 in 2000. By 2050, it will be close to 50.

Typically, growth in the number of old people has two causes. First is the increase in the human lifespan due to better options for medical care, improvements in public health, and better food. Second is the
10   trend for people to have fewer children. This trend is clear from the birthrate, which is the average number of children a woman has. The birthrate needed for a developed country to keep the same population size is about 2.1. Many countries now have birthrates much lower than this. If people don't move to these countries, their populations will fall.

These aging populations will cause problems. The state has a duty to support elderly people through
15   health and social services. As the number of older people increases, more and more services will be needed. At the same time, people in this category will pay little tax. This is because they don't have large incomes. Also, since older people usually spend less on material products than young people, the government's income from sales taxes will be lower. In these ways, the economy will get worse.

Governments can solve the problem of rising costs and falling taxes in two ways. They can reduce the
20   supply of other services, such as education. And they can increase taxes on people with jobs. One feature of an aging population is that the cost of education becomes lower. However, these savings are less than the increase in costs of health and social services.

Not all countries have aging populations. A possible solution to
25   the problems of an aging society is to encourage young people from such countries to live and work there. However, this brings separate problems that are impossible to ignore.

C Identifying topic and main idea

Read the questions below and circle the correct answers according to the text.

1 Which of the following best describes the topic of the text?

    A Falling birthrates

    B Increasing lifespans

    C Aging populations

    D Government services

2 The main idea in each paragraph has a different focus. Match them to the paragraphs. The first one is done for you.

Main idea focus:	Answers	Causes	Facts	Problems	Reactions
Paragraph number:	5	_____	_____	_____	_____

D Finding supporting ideas

1 Work with a partner. In the text, the author makes the claims below. Find two reasons in the text that support each of these claims.

1 People in developed countries are living much longer than they did 150 years ago.

    Reason 1: _____

    Reason 2: _____

2 The aging of society will cause difficulties for governments.

    Reason 1: _____

    Reason 2: _____

3 Older people pay little in taxes.

    Reason 1: _____

    Reason 2: _____

2 Compare your answers with a new partner.

E Making inferences

Which one of the following three opinions would the author probably agree with? Circle the correct answer.

    A Older people will buy more things in the future.

    B In the future, younger people will have to pay more taxes.

    C Older people will have to move to other countries in the future.

Discuss it

Work with a partner or in a small group. Ask and answer the questions below.

1 Look back at the ideas you highlighted. Are they the same? What are the differences?

2 How will a population with more elderly people change your country? Think about these categories:

• advertising	• government spending	• medical care
• entertainment industry	• housing	• roads and transportation
• food	• jobs	• stores

3 Which changes will be good? Which changes will be bad?

4 Find out more

A Information gathering

Work in small groups. Choose one person to take notes in each group.

1 Look at the table of countries and the ages of their populations below. Compare the information. Discuss the questions below.

1 Can you put the countries into two population groups?

2 Which group is your country in?

3 Which country has the highest percentage of children / old people?

4 Which countries face problems with education?

5 Which countries face problems with elderly care?

2 Choose one of the countries. If you were its leader, how would you plan for the future? Give reasons for your answers.

Country	Age / Percentage of population			
	Median	0–14	15–64	65+
Japan	49	12%	58%	30%
Germany	48	13%	64%	23%
South Korea	43	12%	71%	17%
Canada	42	16%	65%	19%
China	38	17%	71%	12%
Argentina	32	24%	64%	12%
Indonesia	31	24%	68%	8%
South Africa	28	28%	66%	6%
Uganda	16	48%	50%	2%

Because ... has ... it will face problems with ...

... has a higher/lower ... than ... so I think ...

If I were the leader in ... I would ...

B Comparing results

Compare your answers with the class. What ideas did you have? Which are the most popular solutions?

One idea we had to help with the problem of ... is ...

A possible solution to the problem of ... is ...

5 Critical thinking

A What does the author mean?

1 Work with a partner. Read the statements below and decide if they are suggested by the text on page 36. Write down your reasons.

Statement	Inference? (Yes/No)	Where (line no.)
1 Electronic devices were not invented 150 years ago.		
2 Younger people go to the doctor as often as older people.		
3 In developed countries, governments will spend more money on education in the future.		

2 Compare your answers with a new partner.

B Ranking

1 As people grow older, many begin to worry about certain things. At what age do you think these worries first appear? Write in the table below.

2 How serious are the worries in your opinion? Write 1 to 5 in the table (1 = least serious; 5 = most serious).

Worry	Age	Ranking	Worry	Age	Ranking
Gray hair or losing hair			Losing strength or movement		
Losing memory			Looking old		
Feeling lonely			Personal safety		
Feeling bored			Money		

3 Compare your answers with a partner. Explain your choices.

C Post your opinion

1 Work in small groups. Discuss the three most serious worries you found above. Do you think they depend on being a man or woman, where you live, or something else?

I think people worry more about ... than ...

In my opinion, women worry about ... more than men.

People in big cities are worried about ...

2 Write a post about what you think old people worry about the most. Give a short reason for your opinion.

D Discussion

1 Work in small groups. In C, you discussed the worries of old people. Now read the questions about society and the elderly below.

    1 What percentage of your salary would you pay to help take care of the elderly?

    2 Are older people kinder than younger people?

    3 Who do you go to for advice? Does age make a difference?

    4 Do older people make better leaders?

    5 Should older people retire so young people can find jobs?

    6 Should parents spend their money before they die, or should they save it for their children?

2 Choose one student to be Student A and one to be Student B. Student A: choose a question and ask Student B. The rest of the group: listen to Student B's answer and then ask follow-up questions.

> In my experience, ...

> Why do you think that ...?

> You can't expect an older person to ...

3 Now agree on a group opinion. Write a summary below.

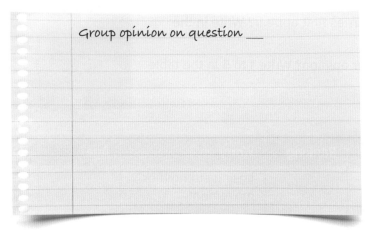

Group opinion on question ___

4 Report your results to the class or another group.

> We didn't all agree, but ...

> Some of us thought that ...

> We all decided that ...

" Quotable quotes
Final thoughts . . . "

Youth is the best time to be rich, and the best time to be poor.

Euripides
Greek writer

1 Why does Euripides say youth is the best time to be rich and poor?

2 Which would you choose—to be rich when young or rich when old? Why?

Do You Want to Live Forever?

FINANCIAL PLANNING

BALDwin

"Find a hobby, like rock-climbing or skydiving. You have to protect yourself from the cost of living too long."

In this unit, you will:

- read an article about living longer.
- read an article about the problems of very long lives.
- discuss the pros and cons of retirement.

1 Critical cartoons

A Warm up

Work with a partner or in a small group. Look at the information on this page and the cartoon. Discuss the questions below.

1 What age would you like to live to? Why?

2 How long do people usually live in your country? How does it compare with other countries?

3 Imagine you are going to live to 150. How does this change your life plans?

4 What is the message of the cartoon? What is the connection to the unit topic?

> I'd like to live to ... because ...

> This changes how long I want to ...

> In my country, I think women live to ...

> This cartoon is making a point about ...

MEDIA link

Groundhog Day (1993) is a well-known comedy movie. It is about a weatherman who lives the same day over and over again. He remembers every day, and in some ways, he feels he is going to live forever. The movie explores the question, "Do you want to live forever?"

For additional media links, go to www.infocus-eltseries.com

2 Core vocabulary

A Skimming and scanning

1 Find and underline the keywords in the text. The first one is done for you. Try to guess their meanings.

Keywords

divide	environmental	extend	gain	pension
principle	proposal	relative	schedule	survive

Living Longer

Jeanne Louise Calment is officially the oldest human being ever. She lived for 122 years and 164 days. She also had a relative, a brother, who lived to age 97. Scientists may someday be able to extend human life much further than that. They believe that we will be able to change our DNA to produce gains of hundreds of years. There are already research proposals to study how to make these changes. 5

But how will this benefit society? All societies are based on the principle that people aren't immortal—we all age and die. We <u>divide</u> our population into groups based on age. Our lifestyles change as we age. For example, people typically retire at around 65 years old and receive a pension until they die. If people live much longer, this retirement schedule will have

to change. Perhaps we will need to consider a person's age compared to their physical condition. For example, a man might be 100 years old but have the physical condition of a 50-year-old. In this case, he may want to continue to work. This could become an economic benefit for society. 10 ... 15

We will also have to think about the environmental cost of a bigger population. Will our world be able to survive if we have to support the millions who want to live a long, long time? 20

2 Which picture goes best with the text? Circle A, B, or C. Then explain your answer to a partner.

A

B
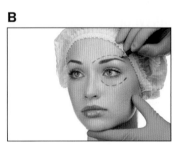

C

B Words in context

Work with a partner. Each pair of sentences below has the same missing keyword. Find which keyword goes with each pair.

1 There is a _____ to build a new sports hall.

Ali made a _____ to take the bus to work rather than drive.

2 The painter _____ his ladder to get to the second-floor window.

If you want to _____ your vacation, ask Ms. Garcia.

3 Elena will receive a good _____ when she retires from the company.

Although Jonah has worked for many years, he won't receive a government _____.

C Word parts: *im*   Example: *immortal*

1 Using the clues below, find words with *im* and do the crossword puzzle. See page 98 or use a dictionary if you need help.

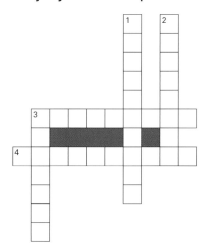

Across

3 Happening or done without waiting; very soon after something else

4 Something that can't happen or be done

Down

1 To stop something or someone from moving

2 Living or lasting forever

3 Not good or right behavior

2 Complete the sentences below with the words from the puzzle. Change the word form as necessary.

1 Extending the human lifespan beyond 125 years is _____.

2 Josh has no _____ plans to retire. He enjoys his job.

3 I believe that it is _____ to help the rich and ignore the poor.

4 Doctors _____ the patient's neck _____ after the accident.

5 We may live long lives in the future, but humans will never become _____.

3 Work with a partner. What do you think *im* means? Circle the correct answer.

A not

B now

C beyond

D Discussion dictation

1 Listen and write down the questions.

1 How old _____ ?

2 Do you _____ ?

3 What things _____ ?

2 Work with a partner. Ask each other the questions. Be sure to ask follow-up questions.

A Pre-reading

1 Quickly scan the text and circle the 10 keywords.

2 What things do people do to live longer?

3 Do many people in your country live to be more than 100? What kinds of lives do they lead?

B Reading

Read the text. Highlight an interesting idea in each paragraph.

 # Can We Afford to Live Longer?

The human lifespan has been extended a lot over the last 100 years. This is especially true in developed countries. The average life expectancy at birth in many of these countries has increased to over 80, and the
5 world average is close to 70. Before modern times, life expectancy was under 40. However, much of the gain since then is due to the decrease in child deaths. The life expectancy of adults hasn't changed as much. For example, a 21-year-old male in sixteenth-century
10 England survived on average for another 50 years, giving him a lifespan of 71 years.

Most cells in the human body are replaced regularly, almost according to a schedule. But over time, cells become damaged. There also seems to be a limit to the
15 number of times a cell can divide. Researchers believe that these are the two reasons for our aging. Currently, there appears to be a limit to the human lifespan of about 120 years.

New medical techniques will probably extend this
20 limit. One technique is to clone* body parts from a close relative to replace parts that become damaged. Another is to change genes** that control aging. Some people have even suggested freezing the body after death. This will create an "ambulance to the
25 future," where we can benefit from new treatments.

Other people believe that we can increase our life expectancy by taking vitamins. Americans now spend more than $50 billion per year on these products. But I say this is a waste of money. Most researchers believe that their only effect is to make the suppliers rich. They say that a
3 more effective proposal for extending life is to exercise, eat a healthy diet, and avoid tobacco and too much alcohol.

Some people will do anything to live even just a few years longer. However, the principle behind trying to live longer is wrong. Already, the health and pension systems
3 of developed countries are under great pressure. If we increase life expectancy further, it will become impossible to care for our old people. In addition, people in developed countries use most of the world's resources. Meanwhile, many people in developing countries don't have enough
4 to eat and have poor healthcare. Our world already faces overpopulation and environmental challenges. We should try to solve these problems, not extend the lifespans of the rich.

*clone (v): to create an exact copy of a plant, animal or living parts
**gene (n): DNA that controls how we grow and develop

C Identifying topic and main idea

Read the questions below and circle the correct answers according to the text.

1 Which of the following best describes the topic of the text?

    A New medical techniques

    B How to live a healthy life

    C Extending human lifespans

    D Overpopulation and the environment

2 Which of the following best describes the main idea of the text?

    A Life extension is possible, but it is not the most important thing.

    B Life extension is impossible for most people.

    C New medical techniques will solve many problems.

    D Taking vitamins increases life expectancy.

D Finding supporting ideas

1 Can human life be extended? Which statement below is true according to the text?

    A It is possible, but it is limited to about 120 years.

    B It is possible if you take the right vitamins.

    C It is possible, but it will cause problems.

    D It is possible, but it will be too expensive.

2 Look back at the text and find information to support your choice. Make notes on the lines.

Line numbers: _____

_____

_____

E Identifying opinions

Which one of the following people agrees with the author?

Ken: Vitamins don't increase a person's lifespan.

Paula: People in developing countries should stop taking vitamins.

Harry: The life expectancy of adults has increased a lot over time.

Discuss it

Work with a partner or in a small group. Ask and answer the questions below.

1 Look back at the ideas you highlighted. Are they the same? What are the differences?

2 How many different stages in life can you identify from 1 to 100 years old? (*baby,* ...)

3 For each of the stages, agree on one or two sentences that best describe it.
For example: *Small babies can't move or talk. They depend on their mothers to feed them.*

4 Find out more

A Information gathering

1 In the table below, order the activities listed from the ones you spend most time doing to the ones you spend least time doing. Write 1 to 10 (1 = most time; 10 = least time).

Activity	Time spent (1–10)	Average time spent in the UK over 80 years
Complaining		
Doing housework		
Eating		
Laughing		
Sleeping		
Using a phone		
Waiting in line		
Watching TV		
Working		

2 Work with a partner. One is Student A; one is Student B. Find out how much time people in the UK spend doing the activities in the table. Student A: ask your partner and write the missing information in the table above. Student B: look at the information in the table on page 98 and answer your partner's questions.

3 Add two more activities that you do regularly to the table. Estimate how much time you will spend doing them over 80 years. Write them in the table.

B Comparing results

Discuss the questions below as a class.

1 The information in the table comes from the UK. What about in your country? Do you think the results might be different? In what ways?

2 The total time for all the activities in the table is about 67 years. What do people do for the other 13 years? Suggest activities.

3 What activities do you and your classmates spend the most time on?

> It's surprising to see that people ...

> I can't believe people spend as much time ...

> I think people in this country spend more/less time ...

> One activity I spend a lot of time doing is ...

5 Critical thinking

A What does the author mean?

1 Work with a partner. Read the statements below and decide if they are suggested by the text on page 44. Write down your reasons.

Statement	Inference? (Yes/No)	Where (line no.)
1 In developing countries, improving children's health will be the most effective way to increase lifespans.		
2 Claims that people can live to 150 years are probably false.		
3 Vitamins are popular in the US.		
4 More money should be spent on how to extend the human lifespan.		

2 Compare your answers with a new partner.

B Ranking

1 What things can affect lifespan? Rank the following from 1 to 4 (1 = very bad, leading to a shorter lifespan; 4 = very good, leading to a longer lifespan). Then compare your answers with a partner.

being married	_____	having good friends	_____
eating fast food often	_____	living in a poor country	_____
eating less	_____	sleeping at least 7 hours a night	_____
exercising regularly	_____	smoking	_____

2 Work with a partner. Think of one more thing that you believe leads to a longer life and one that leads to a shorter life. Share your ideas with your classmates.

C Post your opinion

1 Imagine that scientists have discovered a medicine that makes it possible for people to live to 200. Should the medicine be available for everyone? Read the opinions below and discuss them with a partner.

Longer lives will lead to overpopulation.

If people live longer, it will result in reduced healthcare costs for older people.

Only rich people will be able to live longer.

Only important people should be able to extend their lives.

People who want to extend their lives should pay extra taxes.

2 Now write a post with your opinion.

D Discussion

Situation: Jun and Donna have had successful careers, and their pensions and savings are enough for them to retire on.

Jun: I have worked hard all my life, and now I can finally relax and enjoy myself. Shall I sit by the beach and read books? Go traveling? What shall I do?

Donna: I want to keep busy and help my community. Shall I start a recycling group in my neighborhood? Teach reading skills to people with disabilities? What shall I do?

1 **Work in small groups. Choose A or B. Group A is Jun; Group B is Donna. Make a detailed five-year plan.**

> I've worked hard and paid taxes my whole life. I want to …

> In the first year, I hope to …

> I think that I can help by …

> I've always wanted to …

> By the end of the second year, I want to …

2 **Present your retirement plans to the class.**

3 **Discuss the questions below with your classmates.**

   1 People are living longer. Should they have to retire at a certain age?

   2 How do you think older people can help society?

❝ Quotable quotes
Final thoughts . . . ❞

The quality, not the longevity*, of one's life is what is important.

Martin Luther King Jr.
American activist

1 What is "quality of life"? Think of a definition.

2 Elderly people are sometimes unhappy. What are some reasons for this?

longevity (n): living for a long time

"Go ahead. Click on 'I Am Not A Robot.' I dare you."

I'm not a robot

In this unit, you will:

- read an article about robots in the home.
- read an article about robots as family members.
- work together to design features for a future robot.

1 Critical cartoons

A Warm up

Work with a partner or in a small group. Look at the information on this page and the cartoon. Discuss the questions below.

> I used at least … For example, …

> I'd like to have my own robot because …

1 How many electronic devices have you used in the past 24 hours? What are they?

2 What activities do robots do today? Would you like your own robot? Why or why not?

> I get messages like that when …

3 Have you ever had a message asking to prove you were human? What did you have to do?

> I think the cartoon is making a joke about …

4 What is the message of the cartoon? What is the connection to the unit topic?

MEDIA link

I, Robot (2004) is a science-fiction movie starring Will Smith. It is about how people in the future need robots in their everyday lives.

For additional media links, go to www.infocus-eltseries.com

2 Core vocabulary

1 Find and underline the keywords in the text. The first one is done for you. Try to guess their meanings.

Keywords

adopt	aid	career	code	doubt
effort	force	oppose	potential	serve

Living with Robots

In movies about the future, robots often feature in the home. In some movies, they serve the family by doing housework. In other movies, they may even take the place of family members, acting as lovers or children. But will robots really aid us in our daily tasks in the future? Will people <u>adopt</u> them as their own children?

As with any new technology, some people will oppose robots just because they are new. These people will try to force their opinions on us. They will say, "It is important that we make efforts ourselves. If we don't do our own work, we will become like small children." Others want robots to serve them. They will argue that this gives us the potential to do more because we won't need to do small daily jobs. People will be able to spend more time on their careers and less on housework. And we will have more time for doing fun things.

5

10

15

The potential of robots as family members is more in doubt because robots are only computers that move. A computer code that tells a robot to act like a child is much more difficult to write than one that instructs a robot to wash the dishes. Perhaps the family member most likely to be a robot is the family pet. In fact, several companies have already made different kinds of robot pets. Is the future already here?

20

2 Read the statements below. Which best summarizes the text? Circle A, B, or C. Then explain your answer to a partner.

A In the future, there will be at least one robot serving every home.

B In the future, robots will help us in the home and may become family members.

C In the future, we will all have to buy one or two robots to work in our homes.

B Words in context: identifying a part of speech

1 Five of the keywords are used as nouns. Find them in the text. Match them to the verbs below.

Noun	Verb	Noun
	make	
	gives	
	spend time on	
	is	
	tells	

2 Work with a partner. Choose two keywords from above and make your own sentences. Then compare them with another pair of students.

1 _____

2 _____

C Word parts: *uni*   Example: *universal*

1 Find five words with *uni* in the puzzle and circle them. Check their meanings. See page 99 or use a dictionary if you need help.

2 Complete the sentences below with the words from the puzzle.

1 Rita is a _____ student.

2 The desire for love is _____.

3 The _____ began about 14 billion years ago.

4 East and West Germany were _____ in 1990.

5 At many schools, students must wear a _____.

H	V	F	M	Y	X	J	Z	A	T	D
O	N	P	X	T	D	R	O	M	F	U
N	U	N	I	V	E	R	S	A	L	N
N	K	S	H	Q	O	R	L	U	B	I
U	N	I	F	O	R	M	Y	N	I	V
H	K	G	E	V	H	G	Q	I	N	E
W	G	C	T	B	F	N	P	F	T	R
S	C	H	C	W	Q	V	K	I	H	S
G	U	N	I	V	E	R	S	E	O	I
H	Q	X	R	W	D	O	G	D	J	T
H	T	F	N	V	A	O	C	N	D	Y

3 Work with a partner. What do you think *uni* means? Circle the correct answer.

A to have many parts

B connected with flying

C single or one

D Discussion dictation

1 Listen and write down the questions.

1 Have you seen _____?

2 What role _____?

3 Did the movie _____?

2 Work with a partner. Ask each other the questions. Be sure to ask follow-up questions.

3 Reading skills

A Pre-reading

1 Quickly scan the text and circle the 10 keywords.

2 In what ways will robots make our lives better in the future? In what ways will they make our lives worse?

3 What kinds of robots would you like to see?

B Reading

Read the text. Highlight an interesting idea in each paragraph.

A New Member of the Family

Bill Gates, who made his career in personal computers and writing computer code, believes that the age of home robots has arrived. He compares home robots today with personal computers 40 years ago. At that time, there were large computers in companies and universities, but there were few computers in the home. Gates suggests that soon robots will be adopted in the home in the same way that personal
5   computers have been. This will allow us to live richer lives because robots will do the boring housework.

There are several reasons why the age of home robots is here. First, robots need a brain—a computer. Computing power is now cheap and powerful enough to be this brain. [1] Babies' brains develop quickly. Second, cameras, GPS, artificial intelligence (AI), and voice recognition software let robots react to the world around them. [2] The cost of these systems has fallen quickly, but their power and potential have
10 increased. Finally, as AI progresses, robots will be better at learning from their environment. For example, a robot designed to help around the house will be able to learn about your house, including where you put your food and where you usually forget your keys.

Some people may oppose the idea of robots in every home, but most of us will happily welcome them into our lives. There are many reasons why robots will make our lives better. First, they will provide aid
15 with housework. We will have robots that clean the floor while we are out. Robots will also prepare and serve our meals, and wash and iron our clothes. [3] Others will cut the grass in our garden. Think of all the effort they will save us! We will have time to do the things we love. Second, we can have robot helpers and pets. When we are old, they will remind us to take our medicine, and they will contact emergency services if there is a problem. They will protect us from dangerous people who may try to force their
20 way into our homes. [4] If we are alone, they will keep us company and entertain us. We will come to love them as much as our pets today. But unlike live helpers and pets, they will not die.

25 Home robots may not look like the robots in science-fiction movies, and we might not even think of them as robots. But without a doubt, they will make our lives easier and stop us from being lonely.

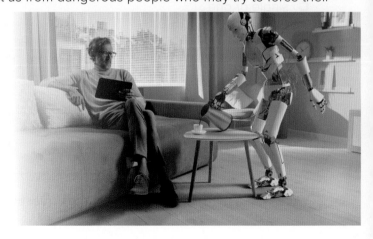

C Identifying topic and main idea

Read the questions below and circle the correct answers according to the text.

1   Which of the following best describes the topic of the text?

    A Computers and robots

    B The danger of robots in the home

    C Robots in the home

    D AI in our lives

2   Which of the following best describes the main idea of the text?

    A Robots will improve our lives in many ways.

    B People oppose robots in the home for many reasons.

    C Home robots will take care of older people.

    D In the future, robots will clean our floors and cut our grass.

D Identifying unnecessary information

1   Look at the four numbered sentences in the text. Which contains information that is not related to the main point of the author?

Sentence number: _____

Reason it is not necessary:_____

2   Compare your answers with a partner.

E Identifying opinions

Which one of the following three opinions would the author probably disagree with?

    A Technology has made our lives busier and more difficult.

    B We will live happier and healthier lives because of modern technology.

    C We will probably love robot pets as much as living ones.

Work with a partner or in a small group. Ask and answer the questions below.

1   Look back at the ideas you highlighted. Are they the same? What are the differences?

2   According to the text, what are some jobs that robots can do today? What jobs will they do in the future?

3   Look at the list of jobs below. Which are you happy for robots or AI to do in the future? Why or why not?

    • airline pilot   • singer

    • cook   • store clerk

    • doctor   • taxi driver

    • police officer • teacher

4 Find out more

A Information gathering

Work with a partner. One is Student A; one is Student B. Student A: use the table below. Student B: use the table on page 99. How many robots in movies and books can you name? Ask your partner for the missing information and complete the table.

Student A

Movie	Robot	Job/Purpose
Alien	Ash	scientist on a spaceship
Star Wars		
Star Trek	Data	officer and scientist
A.I. Artificial Intelligence		
Blade Runner	Pris	personal helper / friend
Forbidden Planet		
RoboCop	ED-209	police officer
Transformers		
Godzilla	Mechagodzilla	sent to destroy the world
Terminator		

B Comparing results

1 Work in small groups. Discuss the questions below.

1 How many of these movies do you know?

2 Can you think of any other movies with robots? If so, what do they look like?

3 Think of the jobs or purposes of the robots. How many of these do you think will come true?

4 Group the movie robots in A into the categories below.

Friendship: _____

Destruction: _____

Knowledge: _____

Protection: _____

Which category will be most important or useful for humans in the future? Why?

2 Share your ideas with the class.

> I know at least …

> There is one movie I saw where …

> I think … will be impossible, even in the future.

> I think the most important type of robot for humans will be … because …

> I'm sure one day there will be …

5 Critical thinking

A What does the author mean?

1 Work with a partner. Read the statements below and decide if they are suggested by the text on page 52. Write down your reasons.

Statement	Inference? (Yes/No)	Where (line no.)
1 There will be many robots in our homes in 40 years.		
2 Cheap computers make robots possible.		
3 Robots will be able to understand what we say and speak with us.		
4 Robots will act as personal healthcare advisers.		

2 Compare your answers with a new partner.

B Ranking

1 How much do you like or dislike the activities below? Which would you like robots to do most? Rank them from 1 to 5 (1 = most; 5 = least).

Activity	Rank (1–5)	Activity	Rank (1–5)
Cleaning the bedroom		Driving a car	
Cleaning the toilet		Getting money from an ATM	
Cooking meals		Paying bills	
Doing homework		Washing dishes	
Doing the laundry		Vacuuming the floor	

2 Compare your answers with a partner. Explain your choices.

C Post your opinion

1 People have different opinions about robots. Read the statements below.

1 Robots can never be equal to humans.

2 If robots are as smart as humans, the laws for them should be the same.

3 Robots and humans should be allowed to marry.

4 We should not be able to buy and sell intelligent robots.

5 Robots should always serve humans.

2 What is your opinion? Choose one of the statements and write a post with your opinion about it.

D Discussion

1 Work in small groups. In C, you wrote about the differences between robots and humans. Now imagine you are inventors in an international robot competition. Work together to design a new robot. Discuss the tasks below in order.

1 Decide what the purpose of the robot is.

> What do we want our robot to do?

> I think it should be able to ...

2 Discuss the features of your robot.

> One of the key features will be ...

> I think it would be cool if ...

3 Draw or describe how it looks.

> The robot looks like ...

> Why don't we try to draw it? Can anybody draw?

4 Give it a name.

> Why don't we call it ...

> That's not a good name. Let's call it ...

5 How much will it cost?

> I think it should cost ...

6 Describe what it can do and how it will communicate.

> Our robot is able to ...

> It will be able to ...

> It will communicate by ...

2 Choose who will present your results to the class. Prepare what you are going to say.

> The robot we are going to present to you is ...

1 Has your computer ever had a virus? What are the most common ways to get a computer virus? How can you prevent it?

2 Do you trust your computer to keep your data safe? Have you ever lost data because of a computer crash? What steps can you take to protect your data?

I Lost My Job to a Machine

"I didn't take anyone's job. This is my company."

In this unit, you will:

- read an article about technology in society.
- read an article about the danger to jobs from new technology.
- discuss ideas for new technology inventions.

1 Critical cartoons

A Warm up

Work with a partner or in a small group. Look at the information on this page and the cartoon. Discuss the questions below.

A lot of factory jobs have gone because ...

One type of job in danger today is ...

I'm a bit worried because ...

I like this cartoon because ...

1 What are some jobs that have gone because of technology? What happened?

2 Are you worried about AI becoming smarter than humans?

3 What jobs today are in danger because of new technology?

4 What do you think of the cartoon? What is the connection to the unit topic?

MEDIA link

In the Age of AI (2019) is a documentary that explores how AI is changing many parts of our lives, from jobs to privacy to international relations.

For additional media links, go to www.infocus-eltseries.com

A Skimming and scanning

1 Find and underline the keywords in the text. The first one is done for you. Try to guess their meanings.

Keywords

application	army	disease	equal	gun
replace	security	union	unlikely	waste

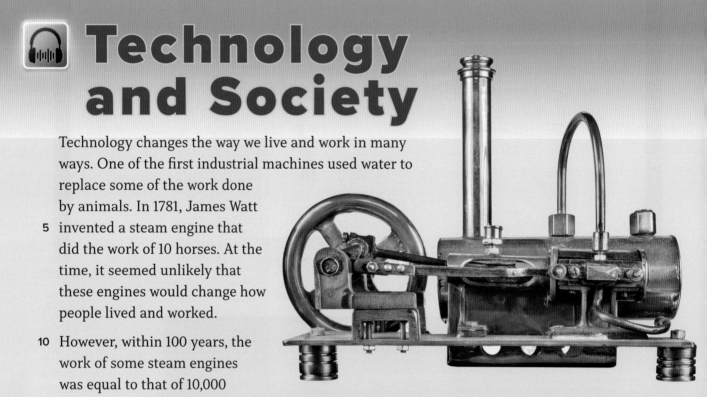

Technology and Society

Technology changes the way we live and work in many ways. One of the first industrial machines used water to replace some of the work done by animals. In 1781, James Watt
5 invented a steam engine that did the work of 10 horses. At the time, it seemed unlikely that these engines would change how people lived and worked.

10 However, within 100 years, the work of some steam engines was equal to that of 10,000 horses. Because of this, fewer farmers were needed on the farms. Workers moved to the city to work in the new factories. At first, life for the workers was difficult. But they got
15 together to form workers' unions and began to fight for better wages and conditions. At the end of the nineteenth century, electricity changed people's lives again, and soon after came automobiles. More recently, computers and smart devices have changed our lives once again.

The next big new technology will be robots using AI. One of the best <u>applications</u> for these robots is in dangerous places. Today, these smart robots help people to provide military
20 security. In the army, they control drones that fly over an enemy and send back information. Some robots can carry guns and fight with soldiers. Robots can also clean up dangerous industrial waste. The waste can cause diseases, such as cancer. Just like steam engines in the past, these new smart robots will also change our lives.

2 Read the statements below. Which best describes the main idea of the text? Circle A, B, or C. Then explain your answer to a partner.

   A Technology has had a big effect on society.

   B Farming became more efficient with the invention of the steam engine.

   C Robots will increase safety in the workplace by doing dangerous jobs.

B Words in context

Work with a partner. Each pair of sentences below has the same missing keyword. Find which keyword goes with each pair.

1 The school's _____ system was very weak, so the students could easily get in and find the test answers.

If you save lots of money when you are young, you can live the rest of your life in financial _____.

2 You should stay away from rats, since they often carry _____.

Many _____ can be cured by modern medicine.

3 The children argued over the cake until their mother cut it into two _____ parts for them to share.

Men and women should have _____ rights in the job place.

C Word parts: *auto*   Example: *automobile*

1 Find five words with *auto* in the puzzle and circle them. Check their meanings. See page 99 or use a dictionary if you need help.

2 Complete the sentences below with the words from the puzzle.

  1 Big Jim got stuck in the _____ doors at Lobstein's Department Store.

  2 A baseball with Shohei Ohtani's _____ sold for $3,000.

  3 Detroit is the center of the _____ industry in the United States.

  4 Amy is using her childhood diaries to write her _____.

  5 Pilots these days fly much of the journey on _____.

O	A	Y	B	A	U	T	O	G	R	A	P	H	G	J
H	H	U	V	Q	I	T	O	L	I	P	O	T	U	A
U	A	Z	T	Q	O	I	Z	G	W	G	W	N	F	S
G	J	D	Z	W	R	X	V	T	U	N	I	N	F	Q
H	B	J	W	N	R	W	O	Z	B	W	L	G	X	O
S	K	O	I	N	A	Y	R	I	K	U	R	X	Z	A
Y	H	P	A	R	G	O	I	B	O	T	U	A	U	C
C	R	J	J	V	D	M	C	V	R	E	B	T	I	D
S	O	W	H	V	T	T	D	V	M	Q	O	T	S	W
K	D	N	S	E	H	Z	O	G	K	M	A	A	V	M
S	D	I	O	B	Q	P	V	D	O	M	X	Q	M	I
I	R	R	T	B	N	J	O	B	O	J	Q	Y	I	B
C	J	W	B	G	O	K	I	T	N	B	W	O	Y	H
Z	C	R	F	A	P	L	U	O	R	U	M	X	X	I
G	T	G	W	A	E	A	G	O	X	J	I	F	I	E

3 Work with a partner. What do you think *auto* means? Circle the correct answer.

  A connected with moving vehicles

  B doing something by yourself or by itself

  C to do with other people

D Discussion dictation

1 Listen and write down the questions.

  1 What kinds _____ ?

  2 How long _____ ?

  3 What difference _____ ?

2 Work with a partner. Ask each other the questions. Be sure to ask follow-up questions.

A Pre-reading

1 Quickly scan the text and circle the 10 keywords.

2 Have you ever ordered food in a restaurant using a tablet computer?

3 How often do you use a barcode reader to scan your shopping at a supermarket?

B Reading

Read the text. Highlight an interesting idea in each paragraph.

The New Luddites?

At the beginning of the Industrial Revolution in England, groups of people called Luddites attacked factories and destroyed machines. They were angry that these machines were taking away jobs. In the 200 years since the Luddites, new technologies have replaced workers in many areas. Labor unions fight against these job losses, but armies of machines are already common in factories, where robots do work in dangerous conditions. This allows
5   people to avoid injury and industrial diseases such as hearing loss due to loud noise. Because of this, there has been an increase in the number of people forced into low-skilled jobs in service industries, such as restaurants and retail stores. [1] New York City has a lot of retail stores. Pay in these jobs is usually low, but at least it gives people work.

Now, a new age of technology in the workplace is being
led by AI. AI is a danger to the job security of people
10   in both skilled and unskilled roles. Unskilled workers
in service industries are now beginning to be replaced
by robots and AI. [2] These days, most banking is done
online or at ATM machines, and we often scan our own
shopping in supermarkets and convenience stores. In
15   many restaurants, we order our food on tablets rather
than directly with waiters. When we shop online, our
orders are packed by robots and will soon be delivered
by drones and self-driving vehicles. AI-powered chatbots
can copy human voices for customer service and phone
20   surveys, and artists and writers are being replaced by AI.
[3] Some of the news you read and images you see online
were probably created by AI.

The blogger Marshall Brain thinks that intelligent robots will soon be equal to or better than humans in many areas, and workers at restaurants and stores will be replaced by robots that will cook and serve our food, throw out waste,
25   and stock shelves at big stores, such as Walmart. [4] The first Walmart opened in 1962. He believes that this change will happen quickly, and tens of millions of workers will have no jobs.

What will happen to these workers who are replaced by robots and AI? In the past, improvements in technology led to increases in job applications for low-skilled work in the service industry. But this is unlikely to happen again. Workers will have nowhere to go since robots and AI will also be doing those low-skilled jobs. Perhaps we will see
30   an era of robot wars, in which new Luddites with guns try to destroy all the robots!

C Identifying topic and main idea

Read the questions below and circle the correct answers according to the text.

1 Which of the following best describes the topic of the text?

    A Robots as weapons

    B The service industry

    C The effects of technology on jobs

    D High unemployment around the world

2 Which of the following best describes the main idea of the text?

    A The service industry will come to an end.

    B Intelligent machines can be dangerous in the workplace.

    C Unemployment will rise among unskilled workers in the future.

    D The lower price of robots in the workplace will make the new Luddites happy.

D Identifying unnecessary information

1 Look at the four numbered sentences in the text. Which two contain information that is not related to the main point of the author?

Sentence number: _____

Reason it is not necessary: _____

Sentence number: _____

Reason it is not necessary: _____

2 Compare your answers with a partner.

E Identifying opinions

Which one of the statements would the author probably agree with?

    A As robots replace working people, those people will find other jobs.

    B The increase in the number of robots in the workplace will lead to social problems.

    C Robots will never replace people in the workplace because they are too expensive.

Work with a partner or in a small group. Ask and answer the questions below.

1 Look back at the ideas you highlighted. Are they the same? What are the differences?

2 In South Korea, they are developing AI English teachers. Could you learn with an AI teacher? Why or why not? Could an AI teacher teach some things better? Are there some things it could not teach?

4 Find out more

A Information gathering

1 Work with a partner. Think of jobs that can be done now or in the future without humans. Look back at the texts on pages 58 and 60 for ideas. Write in the table below.

Type of work	Employer/Workplace
manufacturing	factory

2 With your partner, think of two more types of work where robots or machines can replace humans. If you can, go online to find ideas. Add them to the table.

B Comparing results

Work in small groups. Discuss the questions below.

1 Compare your answers. How many different ideas does your group have?

2 Could robots or AI do the jobs below? Why or why not?

    A prison guard

    B nuclear power station operator

    C astronaut

3 Are there any jobs you think robots shouldn't do? For example, think about these jobs: bus driver, doctor, judge, police officer.

> Robots could be really good/useful as ... because ...

> I don't think AI could/should ever ...

> In my opinion, we should never use robots to ... because ...

> I don't like the idea of robots or AI ...

5 Critical thinking

A What does the author mean?

1 Work with a partner. Read the statements below and decide if they are suggested by the text on page 60. Write down your reasons.

Statement	Inference? (Yes/No)	Where (line no.)
1 Machines in the workplace have always led to unemployment.		
2 AI will replace robots in the workplace.		
3 Robot store clerks will be easier to employ than humans.		
4 Labor unions support machines in factories.		

2 Compare your answers with a new partner.

B Ranking

1 Which kind of jobs are robots and AI most likely to do in the future? Read the list of jobs below and rank them from 1 to 5 (1 = most likely; 5 = least likely).

Job	Rank (1-5)	Job	Rank (1-5)
banker	_____	soldier	_____
caregIver	_____	surgeon	_____
police officer	_____	taxi driver	_____
politician	_____	teacher	_____
receptionist	_____	waiter	_____

2 Work with a partner. Compare your answers and explain your choices.

C Post your opinion

1 Work with a partner. People have different opinions about technology in society. Read the statements below. Ask your partner if he or she agrees with them and why or why not.

1 Technology is great: it makes everything so convenient!

2 Robots and AI are very useful. They do boring jobs, so people can do more interesting things.

3 In the old days, people weren't so lonely. They communicated with other people, not machines.

2 What is your opinion? Choose one of the statements and write a post about it.

D Discussion

1 Work with a partner. In C, you discussed and wrote about the effects of technology on society. Now look at the ideas below for new technology inventions and future life. Discuss these questions about each one:

   1 Do you think the idea is likely to come true?

   2 Would you like to use the invention?

Control machines with your mind
Drive your car with no hands

Nano-robot doctors
No more heart disease

Internet biochip brain implant
Be online all the time

Wall monitors
Use the walls of your home as computer monitors

Packaging you can eat
Wash and eat your yogurt carton

Electric clothes
Charge your phone with your body

TELEPORTING
Work in Sydney, sleep in New York

TIME MACHINE
See friends and relatives who have died

Car speeds controlled by computers
THE END OF TRAFFIC JAMS

Instant language downloads
No more need to learn a language

2 Work in small groups. Compare your ideas. Put each idea into the table below.

Probable	Possible	Impossible

3 Share your ideas with your classmates. Try and agree on a list for the whole class.

> There is a big demand for ... so maybe ...

> Our group agreed that ... is/are quite/very probable.

> The idea of ... is not possible because ...

> We all agreed that the idea for ... is ...

66 Quotable quotes
Final thoughts ... 99

We are stuck with technology when what we really want is just stuff that works.

Douglas Adams
English author

1 Have you ever felt angry when a piece of technology didn't work properly?

2 What technologies have you found to be especially helpful?

"Well, I guess we're the control group."

In this unit, you will:

- read an article about the use of animals in experiments.
- read an article about the pros and cons of using animals for research.
- discuss the idea of ending all animal testing.

1 Critical cartoons

A Warm up

Work with a partner or in a small group. Look at the information on this page and the cartoon. Discuss the questions below.

I think a control group is when ...

I guess companies use animals to ...

I think a lot of people these days ...

Maybe the cartoon shows that ...

1 What is a control group in an experiment? Check online.

2 Why do some companies test new products on animals?

3 More and more companies advertise they do not test on animals. Why?

4 What is the message of the cartoon? What is the connection to the unit topic?

MEDIA link

Test Subjects (2019) is an award-winning documentary. It looks at the pressure on science students to experiment on animals in order to earn their diplomas.

For additional media links, go to www.infocus-eltseries.com

A Skimming and scanning

1 Find and underline the keywords in the text. The first one is done for you. Try to guess their meanings.

Keywords

claim	contract	employee	examine	experiment
issue	parent	patient	refuse	training

Animal Testing

We have used animals in research for as long as scientists have been doing experiments. We have learned many useful things from these experiments. For example, Pavlov's training of dogs helped us understand about learning. University researchers might work to find a cure for   5
patients suffering from a disease. Employees of a cosmetics company may test new makeup. Both use animals to help with their research.

Scientists often have contracts with companies to supply animals for research. These animals can suffer and even   10
die. For example, researchers may give an animal a disease. Then they give medicine to treat the disease. After the medicine begins to work, the animal is killed. Researchers then examine it to see how the medicine was working.

Animal rights supporters do not like this. The issue is   15
whether it is necessary to use animals. Animal rights supporters refuse to believe that animals are necessary. They say there are other ways to do research. But scientists claim they need the animals to get good information. They say that parents of sick children want researchers to use   20
animals if that can make their children better.

2 Read the titles below. Which would also be a good title for the text? Circle A, B, or C. Then explain your answer to a partner.

   A Ending Animal Testing

   B The History of Animal Testing

   C Animal Testing: For or Against?

B Words in context: word friends

1 Work with a partner. Look at the keywords below and the words that go with them. In each case, circle the one word that doesn't go with the keyword.

	Keyword	Word friends			
1	(to) examine _____	**A** effects	**B** a patient	**C** a problem	**D** rest
2	_____ an issue	**A** debate	**B** discuss	**C** give	**D** raise
3	(to) claim _____	**A** about a problem	**B** credit	**C** ownership	**D** to need something

2 Work with your partner. Choose one keyword plus one word friend and make your own sentence. Then read your sentence to another pair of students. Listen and write down their sentence.

Your sentence: _____

Other pair's sentence: _____

C Word parts: *dis*   Example: *disease*

1 Put the sentences below in the right order to make a short story. Try to guess the meaning of any words you don't know.

_____ Some people got sick and died because the research was discontinued.

_____ Other people disagreed with them, but the research was stopped.

_____ Some people disapproved of their experiments and began to complain.

_____ Researchers were looking for a cure for a dangerous disease.

_____ They said we shouldn't disregard the lives of animals, even to help humans.

2 Complete the sentences below with words from the story.

1 Malaria is a _____ that kills millions of people each year.

2 Hiro thinks animal experiments are necessary, but I _____ with him.

3 _____ what I said. I didn't mean it.

4 Mona's parents _____ of her going to the animal rights meeting.

5 Because of some dangerous effects, the medicine was _____.

3 Work with a partner. What do you think *dis* means? Circle the correct answer.

A to be apart from or opposite something

B to be inside something

C to begin doing something

D Discussion dictation

1 Listen and write down the questions.

1 Do you _____ ?

2 Why do you _____ ?

3 Do you think it's OK _____ ?

2 Work with a partner. Ask each other the questions. Be sure to ask follow-up questions.

A Pre-reading

1 Quickly scan the text and circle the 10 keywords.

2 Do you know of any animal experiments? What are they?

3 Some people believe animal testing is wrong. Why do you think they feel this way?

B Reading

Read the text. Highlight an interesting idea in each paragraph.

 # Is Animal Research Necessary?

Many hundreds of years ago, we knew little about the human body. Some people wanted to examine the inside of it to find out how it worked. But, for religious reasons, they couldn't cut up bodies, so they used animals instead.

5 Today, animals are used in many kinds of experiments. Drug companies need to know if a new medicine will work and be safe, so they make a contract with scientists to test it. Scientists can't test it on patients because it may make the patients worse, so they test it on animals. Those animals are often killed, and their bodies are examined to see the effect of the medicine. Animals are also used to find out about diseases. Scientists give animals a disease and then watch them to find out more about the disease. Often, the animals die from the disease, but even if they live, they will be killed and their bodies
10 examined.

Another use of animals is for medical research. For example, to study lack of sleep, mice are placed on a small block in a bucket of water. If they sleep, they slip into the water and wake up,
15 and then climb onto the block again. The mice have to stay awake. Animals are also used for training in medical schools. Students practice on their bodies.

In recent years, experimenting on animals has
20 become an issue that more and more people feel very strongly about. Scientists claim they need to do animal testing. But in my opinion, this isn't true. Most of these tests aren't needed and cause unnecessary pain to animals. Animals, like people, have rights. Animal testing is wrong for several reasons. First, computer models can check the safety of
25 new medicines just as well as animal testing. Second, animal bodies are not the same as human bodies. Using them in tests does not give good information about medicine for humans. Third, it is wrong to cause pain and death to animals. It is cruel to take baby animals from their parents to be used in tests.

People must refuse to use products made by companies that do animal testing. We need to go to the places where companies do animal tests. We must force the employees to set the animals free.
30 Sometimes, we have to break the law. It is time to end animal experiments.

C Identifying topic and main idea

Read the questions below and circle the correct answers according to the text.

1 Which of the following best describes the topic of the text?

    A How the human body works

    B Research into diseases

    C The benefits of animal experiments

    D Animal experiments and animal rights

2 Which of the following best describes the main idea of the text?

    A Animals are used in research, but people are right to complain about it.

    B Animals often suffer because of research and training in medical schools.

    C Many people complain about the pain and death of animals.

    D Animals are not good research subjects.

D Logical reasoning

1 In the text, the author argues against using animals to test medicines. Which of the following statements weakens this argument?

    A Developing medicine using computers is 50 percent faster than using animals.

    B The DNA of chimpanzees is about 98 percent the same as humans, so they are good for testing human medicines.

    C In most societies, people kill and eat animals.

2 Compare your answers with a partner.

E Identifying opinions

Which one of the following people agrees with the author?

Ajay: Experimenting on animals causes suffering, but it is necessary.

Jessica: Animal experiments are wrong and unnecessary.

Sami: Animal rights people should leave animal testers alone.

Discuss it

Work with a partner or in a small group. Ask and answer the questions below.

1 Look back at the ideas you highlighted. Are they the same? What are the differences?

2 Animals are used for many reasons. Look at the list below and write 1 to 5 according to how you feel (1 = most negative about this use; 5 = most positive about this use).

Use

cosmetics	_____	hunting	_____
clothing	_____	medicine	_____
entertainment	_____	pets	_____
food	_____		

3 Compare your answers. Explain your choices.

4 Find out more

A Information gathering

Work with a partner. One is Student A; one is Student B. Student A: use the table below. Student B: use the table on page 100. Ask your partner for the missing information and complete your table.

A: What animals were used for asthma research?

B: Guinea pigs were used for asthma. What was the discovery?

A: Epinephrine.

B: How do you spell that?

Student A

Animals and medical research		
Disease	Animal used	Discovery
Asthma		epinephrine
Diabetes	dog	
Kidney failure		organ transplant
Polio		vaccine
Scarlet fever	mouse	
Smallpox	cow	
Tetanus	horse	

B Comparing results

Discuss the questions below with a partner or in a small group.

1 Which of the above diseases do you know? Look up any you don't know.

2 Have animals been used in the research of any other diseases that you know? Check online to find out more.

3 Some people refuse medicine because of their religion or because they don't agree with animal testing. What do you think of this?

I've never heard of ...

I guess some people ...

We should think about ...

One disease where animals are used is ...

5 Critical thinking

A What does the author mean?

1 Work with a partner. Read the statements below and decide if they are suggested by the text on page 68. Write down your reasons.

Statement	Inference? (Yes/No)	Where (line no.)
1 New medicines aren't usually tested on humans.		
2 Most scientists believe that they don't learn much from the examination of dead animals.		
3 Humans should think about the rights and feelings of animals.		

2 Compare your answers with a new partner.

B Ranking

1 Should some animals have more rights than others? Which animals should have the most rights? Rank the animals listed below from 1 to 6 (1 = most rights; 6 = least rights).

chimpanzees _____   frogs _____

dogs _____   mice _____

flies _____   pigs _____

2 Compare your answers with a partner. Explain the reasons for your ranking.

C Post your opinion

1 Work with a partner. Read the quotes below. Explain them in simple English. Use a dictionary if you need help.

1 *The greatness of a nation and its moral* progress can be judged by the ways its animals are treated.*

Mahatma Gandhi

2 *The time will come when men such as I will look upon the murder of animals as they now do the murder of men.*

Leonardo da Vinci

3 *The use of animals in research is needed to develop new and more effective methods for treating diseases that affect both humans and animals.*

California Biomedical Research Association

*moral: relating to or showing good behavior, fairness, and honesty

2 What is your opinion? Choose one of the quotes and write a post about it.

D Discussion

Work in small groups. You are going to discuss the situation below.

Your government is holding a special meeting about ending all animal testing. A medical researcher, Jinhee, and an animal rights supporter, Matt, are trying to persuade you to support them. Read their arguments.

Matt:	Testing can be done using computer models.
Jinhee:	Computer models can't replace animal testing.
Matt:	Animals are different from humans, so animal testing isn't effective.
Jinhee:	Animals and humans have many of the same health problems and diseases.
Matt:	They should test new medicine on humans, not animals.
Jinhee:	There are many dangers in using humans for testing.
Matt:	There are never any good reasons for animal testing.
Jinhee:	Testing has produced many cures and medicines.
Matt:	Animals have rights.
Jinhee:	Millions of people die from diseases.
Matt:	Animals shouldn't suffer because of human diseases.
Jinhee:	Medical discoveries can stop diseases in pets and other animals.

1 Who do you think makes the best argument? Give your reasons. Decide as a group who you will support.

2 Tell your classmates who you will support and why.

3 Decide as a class who wins your support.

> I trust the opinion of medical researchers / animal rights supporters more than ... because ...

> I think that it's necessary to ... because ...

> We will support ... because ...

> Matt's/Jinhee's argument is weak/strong because ...

❝ Quotable quotes
Final thoughts . . . ❞

If you want to test cosmetics, why do it on some poor animal who hasn't done anything? They should use prisoners who have been convicted of murder or rape instead.

Ellen DeGeneres
Talk show host, actor, writer

1 Do you think it's OK to use prisoners to test cosmetics? Does it depend on the crime?

2 Do you think that some animals should have more rights than murderers?

"I think it stands for, "Please Eat The Activist," which is exactly what I did!"

In this unit, you will:

- read an article about people who support animals.
- read an article about our relationship with animals.
- discuss the different roles animals play for people.

1 Critical cartoons

A Warm up

Work with a partner or in a small group. Look at the information on this page and the cartoon. Discuss the questions below.

1 Do you know what PETA is? Can you guess from the cartoon? Check online.

2 Do you think animals should have rights? Give examples.

3 How important are animal rights in your country?

4 Do you think the cartoon is funny? What is the connection to the unit topic?

> Perhaps PETA is to do with ...

> I think all animals should have some rights, like ...

> In my country, animal rights are ...

> The unit topic and the cartoon are both ...

MEDIA link

Blackfish (2013) is an award-winning documentary. It shows how various sea animals, including orcas, suffered bad treatment at some SeaWorld parks.

For additional media links, go to www.infocus-eltseries.com

2 Core vocabulary

A Skimming and scanning

1 Find and underline the keywords in the text. The first one is done for you. Try to guess their meanings.

Keywords

accuse	basis	feed	generate	murder
prison	protection	release	suffer	suit

Standing Up for Animals

There are two main groups of people today who are against how we treat animals. The first group believes that killing animals is the same as murder. Some in this group even believe that people who eat animals should go to prison. They <u>accuse</u> people who wear animal fur of murder and sometimes attack them. They think that all animals should be released from
5 farms and homes, and they should go where they want. The basis for their belief is that humans are also animals. They feel that the closer other animals are to humans, the worse it is to eat them. They believe we should treat animals differently from other living things like plants.

The second group accepts that we use animals for food, but they oppose anything that
10 makes them suffer. This group feels that modern ways of raising animals are not suited to the animals. They believe that animals should be raised and fed in conditions like those in nature. For example, pigs once lived in forests and ate roots and plants. They are happiest when they have space to run around and protection from subzero weather. But now, pigs are raised in very small areas and fed corn and soybeans. In this small space, they produce a lot
15 of waste. This generates many problems for the pigs' health.

2 Read the titles below. Which would also be a good title for the text? Circle A, B, or C. Then explain your answer to a partner.

   A Vegetarianism

   B Do Animals Have Rights?

   C People Who Care for Animals

B Words in context

Work with a partner. Each pair of sentences below has the same missing word. Find which keyword goes with each pair.

1 Two sisters have been arrested for _____ after police found their dead father.

There were three _____ in the town last year.

2 These papers will form the _____ for our discussion.

Decisions are sometimes made on the _____ of incorrect information.

3 I think he _____ a lot when his wife left him.

If you're not happy with it, you should complain. Don't just _____ in silence.

C Word parts: *sub*   Example: *subzero*

1 Put the sentences below in the right order to make a short story. Try to guess the meaning of any words you don't know.

_____ He was going to explore the Arctic Ocean in a submarine.

_____ Sometimes, Leo feels scared because of thoughts in his subconscious.

_____ He took a subway from his home to an outdoor clothing store.

_____ Yesterday, he found out that he was a substitute for a sailor on an Arctic adventure.

_____ He bought warm clothes because the temperatures would be subzero.

2 Complete the sentences below with words from the story.

1 It's a disadvantage to be very tall if you work in a _____.

2 After the goalkeeper was injured, the manager asked Kyle to be the _____.

3 Mina lost her wallet in the _____ station.

4 _____ temperatures are common in the Canadian winter.

5 Dreams can show our _____ desires.

3 Work with a partner. What do you think *sub* means? Circle the correct answer.

A being above something

B being below something

C being before something

D Discussion dictation

1 Listen and write down the questions.

1 What is _____ ?

2 How is _____ ?

3 What should _____ ?

2 Work with a partner. Ask each other the questions. Be sure to ask follow-up questions.

A Pre-reading

1 Quickly scan the text and circle the 10 keywords.

2 Do you eat meat? Are there any animals that you wouldn't eat? If so, why not?

3 Do you think that it is OK to keep pets in cages?

B Reading

Read the text. Highlight an interesting idea in each paragraph.

People for Animal Rights

Most people agree that it is wrong to cause unnecessary pain to animals. However, we also know that we all suffer pain sometimes. For example, women can suffer great pain when they have babies. For most people, pain is just part of life. For other people, avoiding suffering is the basis of how they think about animals. We can see this when they talk about how we should care for animals. These people
5 claim to support animal rights. At first, it seems that people who want animal rights are good people. They talk about reducing suffering and protecting animals. It is difficult to accuse these people of doing bad things. But that is where their ideas will lead.

I believe that animal rights supporters don't understand the true relationship between
10 animals and humans. All the common farm animals we see today developed from wild animals. Over time, they changed to better suit living with humans. One example of this is how dogs developed from wolves more than 15,000
15 years ago. Some dogs developed to help us hunt better. Other dogs, like sheepdogs, help us take care of farm animals. These farm animals can't survive in the wild. If we released them, most of them would die. They need our protection from

20 bad weather and from wild animals that would kill and eat them. Without us to feed them, they would die of hunger. These animals give us many benefits, but we have to work hard for them.

However, animal rights people want to change our relationship with animals. These people may talk about how farm animals generate waste that causes environmental problems. They may say meat isn't healthy. But for most, the main problem with keeping animals is the pain and suffering. They believe that keeping
25 animals in cages is the same as keeping criminals in prison. A few believe that keeping pets is the same as keeping slaves. Some even say that killing an animal is the same thing as murdering a human being. But if we don't use these farm animals, there is no reason to keep them. The end result is that they will disappear. If a group's actions lead to the loss of an animal species, are those people good?

C Identifying topic and main idea

Read the questions below and circle the correct answers according to the text.

1 Which of the following best describes the topic of the text?

    A Circus animals

    B Unwanted pets

    C Animals as food

    D Treatment of animals

2 Which of the following best describes the main idea of the text?

    A People are cruel to animals in different ways.

    B Animal rights groups are not good for animals.

    C Animals should not be used for entertainment.

    D Pet owners should feel responsible for their animals.

D Logical reasoning

1 In the text, the author argues that we must be careful because more animal rights could lead to farm animals disappearing. Which of the following statements strengthens this argument?

    A Some pigs are raised on factory farms.

    B Raising chickens in factory farms lowers the price of eggs.

    C Factory pig farms generate about 6 liters of waste per animal per day.

2 Compare your answers with a partner.

E Identifying opinions

Which one of the following people disagrees with the author?

  Ana: I think people have the right to use animals in whatever way they want.

  Melisa: I believe that there is a big difference between taking care of animals and giving them rights.

  Zak: Animals are not ours to eat, wear, experiment on, or use for entertainment.

Work with a partner or in a small group. Ask and answer the questions below.

1 Look back at the ideas you highlighted. Are they the same? What are the differences?

2 What, if anything, makes humans special or different from animals?

3 Einstein and Gandhi were both vegetarians. Could you be a vegetarian?

4 Find out more

A Information gathering

Work with a partner. One is Student A; one is Student B. How many plants and animals are used each year to feed humans? Ask your partner for the missing information and complete the table.

Student A: use the table below. Student B: use the table on page 100.

> How many kilograms of chicken are produced for each person in the USA?

> About 55 kilograms. How many kilograms are produced in China?

Student A

Food production (in kilograms per person per year)					
Product	China	France	Japan	UK	USA
Chicken	9.2	17.8	10.9	22.2	
Corn (maize)	144.3		0.0	0.0	1,002.3
Cow	4.6	26.3	3.9		
Cow's milk		374.1	59.1	227.2	284.2
Horse	0.1	0.1		0.1	0.2
Pig	38.6		10.0	12.1	28.3
Potato	66.1	122.8	18.6		61.8
Rice		2.0	66.4	0.0	26.8
Soybean	10.8	1.9		0.0	265.6

B Comparing results

Discuss the questions below with a partner or in a small group.

1 Which information surprised you? Why?

2 What explanations can you give for this data?

> I didn't realize that ...

> I was surprised to see that ...

> It's easy to explain why ...

> One reason for this figure could be ...

> What I can't understand is ...

5 Critical thinking

A What does the author mean?

1 Work with a partner. Read the statements below and decide if they are suggested by the text on page 76. Write down your reasons.

Statement	Inference? (Yes/No)	Where (line no.)
1 The way we keep animals today is much worse than in the past.		
2 Humans and animals have developed a relationship in which we depend on each other.		
3 We support animals if we go to shows and watch them do tricks.		

2 Compare your answers with a new partner.

B Ranking

1 What makes an animal popular? Rank the following animals from 1 to 7 (1 = most liked; 7 = least liked). Then write your image of each animal.

Animal	Ranking (1–7)	Description of image
Bear		
Dog		
Monkey		
Panda		
Rabbit		
Shark		
Snake		

2 Compare your answers with a partner. Give reasons for your choices.

C Post your opinion

1 The circus was coming to town, but it was canceled because of animal rights people. Read the social media comments about this.

2 What is your opinion? Write a post about it.

What a shame. I was looking forward to it. Why do some people always have to spoil the fun?

This makes me happy. I hate to see animals in cages.

Why don't they complain about important things, like homeless people?

D Discussion

In C, you wrote about what animal rights supporters did. Now imagine what other people think about animals.

1 Work in small groups—if possible, in groups of five. Choose one of the roles below for your group. Then read and discuss the statements below. Make notes as you discuss.

A  **B**  **C**  **D**  **E**

| Pet store owner | Farmer in developing country | Vegetarian | Vet | Butcher |

1 A lot of people depend on animals for their jobs. Using animals is natural.

2 We should treat all animals with care and respect. Humans are animals too.

3 It's hard enough just to make a living for my family. I can't worry about animal rights.

4 Feeding animals for meat uses more resources than just growing vegetables to eat. It's too wasteful.

5 Although selling pets sometimes causes them pain and suffering, the joy that these animals give to their owners is more important.

6 It's important that meat isn't too expensive. But the animals must live in good conditions, and their deaths must be as painless as possible.

2 Share your group's opinions with the class. Students who are listening should ask follow-up questions.

> In our opinion, people are more important than animals because ...

> We are pet store owners. We thought that ... However, ...

> We think people who complain about ... are foolish because ...

> We believe that nobody has the right to ...

" Quotable quotes
Final thoughts . . . "

Hunting is not a sport. In a sport, both sides should know they're in the game.

Paul Rodriguez
Mexican-American comedian and actor

If God hadn't wanted us to eat animals, he wouldn't have made them so darn* tasty!

Stephen Colbert
American writer, comedian, and TV host

1 Explain what the quotes are saying.

2 How do they relate to the topic of this unit?

*darn (adj., informal): very

Online (Dis)Information

"I just feel fortunate to live in a world with so much disinformation at my fingertips."

In this unit, you will:

- read an article about Large Language Models (LLMs).
- read an article about the advantages of LLMs.
- discuss issues related to using LLMs.

1 Critical cartoons

A Warm up

Work with a partner or in a small group. Look at the information on this page and the cartoon. Discuss the questions below.

1 What does the phrase "at my fingertips" mean? Check online.

2 What websites do you use to find information? Which are best? Why?

3 Does your school or teacher have any rules about going online to find information?

4 What is the message of the cartoon? What is the connection to the unit topic?

> I think it means ...

> One of my favorite websites is ...

> One rule my college has is ...

> I think the point of this cartoon is ...

MEDIA link

The Age of AI (2019) is an original YouTube series hosted by actor Robert Downey Jr. It explores the world of AI and how it may affect society.

For additional media links, go to www.infocus-eltseries.com

A Skimming and scanning

1 Find and underline the keywords in the text. The first one is done for you. Try to guess their meanings.

Keywords

aware	contribution	debate	define	editor
legal	property	shift	survey	user

The Shift to Large Language Models

The world of information is changing. This change, or shift, is happening because of something called Large Language Models, or LLMs. LLMs are a kind of computer program, and they are changing how we get information in the digital age. ChatGPT is one example.

How do LLMs work? Think of them as smart editors. They can read and understand texts, define words, and then they can write new texts. They can answer questions, give summaries, 5 and even help users create things. They do this by using a lot of data; they use it to learn. But this data is the property of others.

People are becoming more <u>aware</u> of LLMs and how they are changing things. Some people think these changes are good. LLMs make it easier to find and use 10 information. They also make a big contribution to work and study. A user can ask an LLM a question and get an answer quickly. That is all very useful.

But there is also a debate about LLMs. Are they legal? Who should control them? Who should have access 15 to them? Who should have access to them? Can we trust the information they provide? A recent survey showed that many people are unsure about these questions. It seems we have to think about these LLMs more carefully.

2 Read the statements below. Which best summarizes the text? Circle A, B, or C. Then explain your answer to a partner.

A LLMs are large and powerful computers.

B LLMs help people find and use information.

C LLMs are probably not legal.

B Words in context: word friends

1 Work with a partner. Look at the keywords below and the words that go with them. In each case, circle the one word that doesn't go with the keyword.

Keyword	Word friends			
1 _____ editor	**A** newspaper	**B** dictionary	**C** word	**D** magazine
2 _____ a survey	**A** take	**B** according to	**C** write	**D** conduct
3 legal _____	**A** crime	**B** secretary	**C** action	**D** argument

2 Work with your partner. Choose one keyword plus one word friend and make your own sentence. Then read your sentence to another pair of students. Listen and write down their sentence.

Your sentence: _____

Other pair's sentence: _____

C Word parts: *sur*   Example: *survey*

1 Find five words with *sur* in the puzzle and circle them. Check their meanings. See page 101 or use a dictionary if you need help.

2 Complete the sentences below with the words from the puzzle.

1 On December 25, ice formed on the _____ of the lake.

2 The fuel _____ almost doubled the price of the airline ticket.

3 Please write your _____ on the line at the bottom of the form.

4 _____ all other athletes, Veronica's jump set a new record.

5 Brian bought his hat in an army _____ store.

S	U	R	P	A	S	S	I	N	G
F	C	S	N	S	P	D	A	M	L
S	Z	S	U	U	S	W	H	E	B
U	A	U	O	R	L	C	B	Z	K
R	A	R	A	C	F	M	R	L	H
P	U	N	X	H	L	A	W	F	O
L	K	A	U	A	T	M	C	I	E
U	N	M	D	R	C	U	H	E	E
S	W	E	Y	G	P	Y	Z	Q	I
B	R	U	T	E	E	D	N	B	P

3 Work with a partner. What do you think *sur* means? Circle the correct answer.

A under

B connected with shopping

C beyond or extra

D Discussion dictation

1 Listen and write down the questions.

1 Have you _____ ?

2 Do you _____ ?

3 How has _____ ?

2 Work with a partner. Ask each other the questions. Be sure to ask follow-up questions.

3 Reading skills

A Pre-reading

1 Quickly scan the text and circle the 10 keywords.

2 Imagine you are going to write a report for your teacher in English. Which of the following do you think is OK?

- Ask a native-speaker friend to help you write the report.
- Ask a native-speaker friend to check the report.
- Use a computer program such as ChatGPT to write the report.
- Use a computer program such as ChatGPT to check the content of the report.
- Use a computer program such as ChatGPT to check the grammar of the report.

3 Which of the above strategies have you used before? Explain to a partner.

B Reading

Read the text. Highlight an interesting idea in each paragraph.

 # Our Smart Best Friends

Imagine you have a friend who knows all the books in the world. This friend can help you with many things. This is not a dream, but real life today. We have this friend in the form of Large Language Models (LLMs).

LLMs are very smart computer programs. They can read and appear to understand a lot of information from books, articles, and the internet. It is like they own a big property of knowledge. They learn from
5 what people write and say around the world. Because of this, they can help us in many surprising ways.

LLMs are making a big contribution to our lives. For example, they can help a person write a book or an article. If you are a writer or an editor, you can ask an LLM for ideas. The LLM will give you many ideas because it has read and learned a lot of things.

LLMs are also helping us with legal work. Lawyers can use them to
10 understand difficult laws. LLMs can read and understand all the legal books in the world. So, they can give very good advice to lawyers.

LLMs can even write computer programs! If you are an LLM user who wants to make a computer program, you can ask an LLM for help. It will show you how to write the program. This is a very big shift in how we make
15 computer programs.

LLMs aren't just useful for experts—they can help everyone. For instance, they can help us check and fix writing mistakes. They can even help us write our own stories or articles. They can offer ideas or write a complete piece for us.

LLMs can also survey a large amount of information extremely quickly. They can read and understand
20 more books in a few seconds than a human can read in a year. This speed can make a big difference when we need to find something quickly.

Many people are aware of the power of LLMs. They say they are very helpful and make their work easier. We are still learning about all the things they can do. In the debate about computer power, LLMs are one of the most exciting things. They have already changed how we do many things. They will keep helping
25 us in new and surprising ways, but we will need to define the role LLMs play. Their power to understand and use information is an important step forward in the world of technology.

C Identifying topic and main idea

Read the questions below and circle the correct answers according to the text.

1 Which of the following best describes the topic of the text?

    A Surveying information

    B The new world of LLMs

    C The future of editors

    D The debate around computer power

2 Which of the following best describes the main idea of the text?

    A LLMs are useful for lawyers.

    B LLMs will become our friends.

    C LLMs are an exciting new technology.

    D LLMs can predict the future of technology.

D Finding supporting ideas

1 Work with a partner. In the text, the author lists five ways that LLMs can help us. List those ways below. The first one has been done for you.

    1 *They can help a person write a book or an article.*

    2 _____

    3 _____

    4 _____

    5 _____

2 Compare your answers with a new partner.

E Identifying opinions

Which one of the following statements would the author probably agree with?

    A LLMs can help us understand difficult laws.

    B LLMs won't have much influence on our digital future.

    C LLMs are stealing other people's information.

Discuss it

Work with a partner or in a small group. Ask and answer the questions below.

1 Look back at the ideas you highlighted. Are they the same? What are the differences?

2 If you were ill, would you use ChatGPT or some other LLM to look up medical information? Would you follow the advice given?

3 What other businesses are changing because of LLMs? Think about computer software, education, customer service, translation, job searches, etc. How are they changing?

4 Find out more

A Information gathering

1 Interview a partner. In the last month, how often has your partner done the activities below? Did he or she use a website or an app? Fill out the table.

Internet activity	Number of times done in previous month			Using a website or app	
	1-10	11-30	>30	Website	App
Translated text from one language to another					
Used YouTube to study English					
Used a search engine to generate ideas					
Used a search engine to do research for a report					
Used a search engine to reserve a plane ticket					
Used a search engine to find the cheapest price for a product					
Studied English vocabulary					
Used the internet to write computer code					
Used the internet to check facts					

How many times have you … in the last month?

What did you use to …?

B Comparing results

Work in small groups. Discuss the questions below.

1 Which were the most popular activities?

2 Are there any other internet activities like those that are currently popular? What are they?

3 How do you feel when you can't find information online? What do you do?

The most popular activities in our group were …

Another popular thing to do online is …

When we can't find information online, some of us …

5 Critical thinking

A What does the author mean?

1 Work with a partner. Read the statements below and decide if they are suggested by the text on **page 84**. Write down your reasons.

Statement	Inference? (Yes/No)	Where (line no.)
1 You are a writer. LLMs are a good way to get an idea for a new book.		
2 LLMs can teach you how to write computer code.		
3 LLMs sometimes make grammar mistakes.		
4 We don't know all the things that LLMs can do.		
5 LLMs will make us all more intelligent.		

2 Compare your answers with a new partner.

B Ranking

1 What makes an information source good? Think about the information sources below. Which do you trust the most? Write 1 to 5 on the lines below (1 = most trusted; 5 = least trusted).

blog _____   ChatGPT _____

Facebook _____   TV _____

Google _____   Wikipedia _____

magazine _____   TikTok _____

newspaper _____   Other: _____

radio _____   _____ _____

2 Compare your answers with a partner. Explain your choices.

C Post your opinion

1 Are library research skills taught in schools in your country? What about internet research skills? Read the statements below.

1 LLMs such as ChatGPT save me time when I do research.

2 Human experts are always more reliable than AI.

3 Lazy students use LLMs.

4 Free is not always good.

5 Copying and pasting from the internet for a school report is fine.

2 What is your opinion? Choose one of the statements and write a post about it.

D Discussion

In C, you wrote about research skills and using LLMs to find information. Now you are going to discuss the right to use that information.

1 Work in small groups.

Group A: you are representatives of a group of publishers of textbooks, novels, and other works.
Group B: you are students who want to use LLMs to do research and write reports.
Group C: you work for an internet search engine that uses LLM results in its search results.
Group D: you are teachers. More and more students are using LLMs to write reports.

Choose A, B, C, or D. Discuss each of the statements below from your group's point of view. Then write a short summary of your opinions.

1 LLMs use text data, including books, to learn. They should pay the writers and publishers of those books.

2 Students should not be allowed to use LLMs when writing reports for school.

3 LLMs are just a new way of searching data. They should be free for everyone.

4 Students who submit reports created by LLMs should be expelled.*

5 LLMs shouldn't use a text unless the owner of that text has given permission.

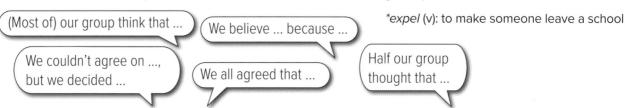

(Most of) our group think that ...

We believe ... because ...

*expel (v): to make someone leave a school

We couldn't agree on ..., but we decided ...

We all agreed that ...

Half our group thought that ...

2 Report your results to the class or another group using your notes. Students who are listening should ask a follow-up question and write the answer below.

Follow-up question	Answer

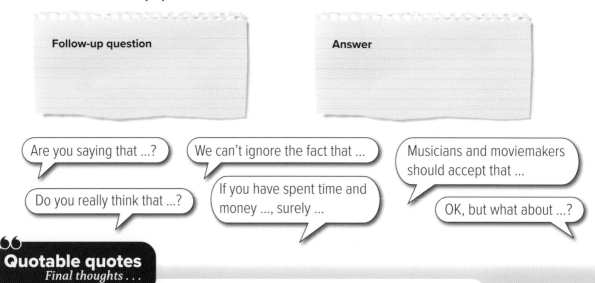

Are you saying that ...?

We can't ignore the fact that ...

Musicians and moviemakers should accept that ...

Do you really think that ...?

If you have spent time and money ..., surely ...

OK, but what about ...?

66 Quotable quotes
Final thoughts . . . 99

AI is probably the most important thing humanity has ever worked on. I think of it as something more profound* than electricity or fire.

Sundar Pichai
CEO of Alphabet Inc., parent company of Google

1 In what ways have electricity and fire benefited humanity?

2 Do you think AI will help humanity more than electricity or fire?

*profound (adj): deep, strong, powerful

I'M YOUR PHONE — I FEED YOU FILTERED OPINIONS TO REINFORCE THOSE YOU ALREADY HAVE

CHRIS MADDEN

reinforce (v): to make something stronger

PHONEY WORLD VIEW

In this unit, you will:
- read an article about the history of online information.
- read an article about LLMs and fake news.
- discuss news and citizen journalism.

1 Critical cartoons

A Warm up

Work with a partner or in a small group. Look at the information on this page and the cartoon. Discuss the questions below.

1 What does the word "phony" mean? Look it up in a dictionary. Why do you think the artist uses the spelling "phoney" instead?

2 What are the main newspapers and radio and TV stations in your country? What are the biggest media companies?

3 How often do you watch the news on TV? What other ways do you get the news?

4 What is the message of the cartoon? What is the connection to the unit topic?

> The word "phony" means ... I think it's "phoney" in the cartoon because ...

> The main media companies in my country are ...

> I usually get the news ...

> I think the cartoon's message is ...

MEDIA link *The ChatGPT Revolution* (2023) is a CBS Reports YouTube documentary. It explores how AI tools such as ChatGPT have changed the world overnight. It also discusses some of the possible dangers.

For additional media links, go to www.infocus-eltseries.com

A Skimming and scanning

1 Find and underline the keywords in the text. The first one is done for you. Try to guess their meanings.

Keywords

commit	despite	document	finance	host
penalty	refer	rely	source	vote

Online Information: A Brief History

In the past, if we wanted to learn something, we would read books or ask people. But in 1991, the first website was made, and it changed how we find information. We could find facts by typing into a computer. We could refer to many sources and different documents. We could use online dictionaries and online encyclopedias, like Wikipedia, for quick answers.

Websites like Wikipedia host articles on millions of different topics. People all around the world regularly <u>commit</u> some of their time to write and update these articles. But despite this, not all the information is true. We must be careful.

Now, we have something even more powerful. Large Language Models (LLMs), like ChatGPT, have come into our lives. These LLMs are very powerful tools and sources of information. They can write essays, answer questions, and even write computer programs. They are financed by technology companies who believe LLMs will change the world. But can we rely on the information they provide?

5

10

15

Just like we vote for our leaders because we trust them, we must also be able to trust the information provided by LLMs. LLMs have made finding information very fast and easy, but there are no penalties for providing false information. Perhaps that should change.

2 Which picture best illustrates the main idea of the text? Circle A, B, or C. Then explain your answer to a partner.

A

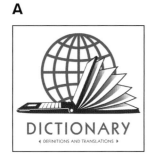

B

C

B Words in context

Work with a partner. Each pair of sentences below has the same missing word. Find which keyword goes with each pair.

1 He was sent to prison for a crime that he didn't _____.

In some countries, people who _____ murder are given the death penalty.

2 The doctor _____ to the patient's smoking and drinking, and told him to quit both.

If you want to know when the next train leaves, you should _____ to the schedule.

3 Money is often a _____ of disagreement for young married couples.

Oranges are a good _____ of vitamin C.

C Word parts: *inter*   Example: *internet*

1 Find five words with *inter* in the puzzle and circle them. Check their meanings. See page 101 or use a dictionary if you need help.

2 Complete the sentences below with the words from the puzzle.

1 All _____ flights are now non-smoking.

2 The parts of these toys are _____.

3 David and Mika are arguing again, but let's not _____.

4 America has almost 80,000 kilometers of _____ highways.

5 Hugo enjoys reading the news on the _____.

O	N	S	I	B	E	O	B	H	W	C	J	V	W	V
Z	C	D	T	C	C	S	K	P	O	K	F	G	P	S
I	N	T	E	R	C	H	A	N	G	E	A	B	L	E
T	G	F	L	O	J	R	D	K	Y	B	M	J	W	L
F	I	Y	N	K	T	P	O	L	B	D	B	N	K	I
I	F	N	C	D	L	K	Q	Z	T	I	E	D	I	F
N	R	S	T	E	C	X	C	S	J	X	J	X	I	I
T	I	N	T	E	R	N	A	T	I	O	N	A	L	N
E	L	B	J	A	R	N	T	F	Q	W	Q	C	P	T
R	S	V	X	W	Y	F	F	E	R	Z	I	U	Y	E
S	M	M	H	J	V	H	E	R	I	I	C	J	X	R
T	W	Q	P	U	H	R	J	R	B	M	I	X	M	N
A	Q	B	E	P	L	A	O	Z	E	O	V	I	L	E
T	C	B	U	M	E	F	M	A	V	B	W	E	T	T
E	G	F	H	O	F	W	E	I	C	U	W	C	K	V

3 Work with a partner. What do you think *inter* means? Circle the correct answer.

A something very long

B between or among something

C on top of something

D Discussion dictation

1 Listen and write down the questions.

1 How often _____?

2 What type of _____?

3 Are there any _____ ?

2 Work with a partner. Ask each other the questions. Be sure to ask follow-up questions.

③ Reading skills

A Pre-reading

1 Quickly scan the text and circle the 10 keywords.

2 Do you find news on the internet interesting or boring? Why?

3 What is a recent news story you saw or heard about that you think is probably fake? What was the news source?

B Reading

Read the text. Highlight an interesting idea in each paragraph.

Misinformation Highways

When we use the internet, we often find ourselves clicking on eye-catching headlines. Imagine you are on your favorite social media platform, looking at different posts. Suddenly, you see a news article headline that grabs your attention. It is hosted on a website you don't know. The headline is shocking, so you click on it. This is where Large Language Models (LLMs) can play a role. They can create
5 interesting content that makes us click.

Big tech companies finance the development of LLMs because they believe LLMs will change the world. But we need to be careful because not all the information we read online is true. In fact, much is fake. LLMs can write stories that seem true—but they are not.

People sometimes believe in strange, fake stories. According to a survey from 2019, approximately
10 one-third of Americans believe that aliens are already visiting Earth from other planets. They think that the US government is hiding this information. Another example of fake news is the idea that 5G networks created the COVID-19 pandemic.

LLMs are very good at making documents with statements that seem true. However, it is easy for people to use LLMs to write fake news. This could trick people who rely on these sources for
15 information. Fake news can have a serious effect, like changing how people vote in an election.

Even though there are laws against spreading fake news, the penalty is often not big enough to stop people or companies. And although there are legal systems in place, it is difficult to make sure people follow the law on the internet. It is hard to know who is responsible if fake news is made by an LLM and then referred to and shared by people who may not know it is not true. Also, many people share news
20 on social media without checking if it is true or not. This and LLMs' ability to write fake or misleading information can lead to such news spreading fast. Some people may even commit crimes based on this fake or misleading information.

So, despite the amazing things LLMs can do, we need to be aware of the dangers. There is a big debate about
25 how to deal with this issue. As users of the internet, we should be a part of this discussion. We need to decide how we want to manage our online information in the future. We need to find a balance. LLMs can help us in many ways, but we also need to control the risks. If
30 we can do so successfully, we can make sure that the internet is a place for finding true and useful information.

C Identifying topic and main idea

Read the questions below and circle the correct answers according to the text.

1 Which of the following best describes the topic of the text?

    A Social media
    B The internet
    C Big tech companies
    D Fake news

2 Which of the following best describes the main idea of the text?

    A There is a risk in relying on the internet for news.
    B People learn a wide range of things from the internet.
    C A lot of people believe strange things.
    D News today is often shocking.

D Finding supporting ideas

1 Work with a partner. In the text, the author made the three claims below. Find two reasons that support each of these claims.

    1 Many people believe fake news.

        Reason 1: _____

        Reason 2: _____

    2 It is difficult to prevent the spread of fake news.

        Reason 1: _____

        Reason 2: _____

    3 Fake news spreads quickly.

        Reason 1: _____

        Reason 2: _____

2 Compare your answers with a new partner.

E Identifying opinions

Which one of the following people agrees with the author?

    Leila: Large internet companies never publish fake news.
    Rick: Fake news can have a negative effect on society.
    Judy: Most of the news written by LLMs is fake.

Work with a partner or in a small group. Ask and answer the questions below.

    1 Look back at the ideas you highlighted. Are they the same? What are the differences?

    2 What news stories interested you last week? Why did you find them interesting?

    3 How can you judge if the online news you read is true?
        Think about:
        • comparing stories
        • who the author is
        • which news organization it is

4 Find out more

A Information gathering

1 Work with a partner. Look at the different types of news stories and headlines below. Match the headlines to the types. Write in the table below.

Business	Education	*Entertainment*
FASHION	*Health*	**Politics**
Science	**SPORT**	Technology

Headline	Type of news
1 New Record in Women's Marathon	
2 Ben and Jennifer Back Together	
3 Stock Market Slides Again	
4 Trump Aims for the White House	
5 Mini Black Hole Discovered Close to Earth	
6 Designer Wins Big Award	
7 Internet Companies Fight Privacy	
8 Five Foods for the Brain	
9 University to Use AI Teachers	
10	
11	
12	

2 What do you think each story is about? Which stories would you be interested in?

> The headline ... could be / is probably about ...

> I think ... must be to do with ... because ...

3 Choose your favorite three types of news stories. Think of a recent headline for each. Write them in the table. What is your news source for each story?

B Comparing results

Work in small groups. Discuss the questions below. Then share your ideas with the class.

1 Which news stories are the most popular?

2 Compare the headlines you wrote. Which are the most interesting?

3 Which are the most popular categories? What sources of news are popular?

> We all liked reading ... stories.

> The most popular source for news for us was ...

> The most interesting headline in our group was ...

> Most of us enjoy ... kind of stories.

5 Critical thinking

A What does the author mean?

1 Work with a partner. Read the statements below and decide if they are suggested by the text on page 92. Write down your reasons.

Statement	Inference? (Yes/No)	Where (line no.)
1 LLMs could have a negative effect on society.		
2 Shocking headlines attract our attention.		
3 The US government has evidence of alien visitors.		

2 Compare your answers with a new partner.

B Ranking

Work with a partner. Here are six headlines. Put them in order (1 = most probably true; 6 = least probably true). Explain your reasons.

Headline	How probable (1–6)
NEWBORN BABY CAN TALK	_____
WOLF APPEARS IN SUPERMARKET	_____
MAN MARRIES HIS TWIN BY MISTAKE	_____
FARMER'S PUMPKIN BIGGER THAN HIS CAR	_____
COMPUTER WRITES BEST-SELLING NOVEL	_____
WOMAN LIVES ON LIGHT AND AIR FOR SIX MONTHS	_____

This can't be true because ...

This sounds strange to me. I don't think ...

It might be possible, but ...

That's impossible!

C Post your opinion

1 Read the unusual news headlines.

TWELVE-YEAR-OLD HEADS TO HARVARD UNIVERSITY

UFO CRASHES INTO MOUNTAIN

CHIMPANZEE LEARNS TO TALK

2 What is your opinion about these stories? Are there any unusual news stories like these in your country? Choose one of the above or one of your own and write a post about it.

D Discussion

In C, you wrote about unusual new stories. Often, these stories are fake news, but not always. Now read about a very unusual but true story.

In 2009, a plane crash-landed on the Hudson River near New York. Amazingly, nobody was hurt. But the story and photos were on the internet on blogs and social networking sites long before it reached the mass media. The reporters were not traditional journalists but "citizen journalists."

1 Work in small groups. Discuss the differences between traditional reporting and citizen journalism. Write your ideas in the table below.

	Traditional reporting	Citizen journalism
1 Technologies used	printing, ...	
2 Reported when		immediately
3 Reported where		
4 Reported by whom		
5 Good points		
6 Bad points		

2 "One day, most news will come from citizen journalists." In your groups:

• Collect arguments for and against this idea.

• Write a summary of your group's ideas.

3 Report your ideas to the class. Add your classmates' ideas to your summary. Then use your notes to discuss the good and bad points about citizen journalists.

> They are not controlled by ...

> They cover stories that professional journalists can't ...

> They can be inaccurate because ...

> They don't report to ...

> They aren't trained, so ...

Quotable quotes
Final thoughts . . .

Whoever controls the media, controls the mind.

Jim Morrison
Lead singer of rock band The Doors

1 Who controls the media in your country?

2 In what ways can people's minds be controlled?

Activities

Unit 1, page 3, Core vocabulary

C Word parts

Answers: words with *ism*

atheism   communism   consumerism   feminism   terrorism

Unit 2, page 11, Core vocabulary

C Word parts

Answers: words with *con/com*

combine   compact   company   contemporary   convenient

Unit 4, page 30, Find out more

A Information gathering

Student A: use the table below. Ask your partner for the missing information and complete the table.

Competition	Situation	Result
1 Apple v. Google		
2 Lewis Hamilton v. Nico Rosberg	Lewis Hamilton and Nico Rosberg were Formula 1 race drivers on the same team. During the 2014 Belgian Grand Prix race, Rosberg's car hit Hamilton's car, causing damage, and Hamilton had to retire from the race.	Rosberg finished second in the race, but many people believed Rosberg hit Hamilton on purpose. After the race, people showed their disapproval of Rosberg's action. Hamilton said Rosberg admitted to hitting him on purpose.
3 Scott v. Amundsen		
4 USSR v. USA space race	During the 1960s, the Union of Soviet Socialist Republics (USSR) and the United States were in a space race. They were competing to be the first to put a man in space and on the moon.	On April 12, 1961, Russian Yuri Gagarin became the first man in space. On July 20, 1969, the American Neil Armstrong became the first person to walk on the moon.

Unit 5, page 35, Core vocabulary

Answers: words with *medi*

median   mediate   medieval   mediocre   Mediterranean

Unit 5, page 36, Reading skills

A Pre-reading

Answers

Country	Life expectancy
Argentina	77
Ethiopia	68
Germany	82
Japan	85
Russia	73
South Africa	65
USA	79

Unit 6, page 43, Core vocabulary

C Word parts

Answers: words with *im*

immediate   immobilize   immoral   immortal   impossible

Unit 6, page 46, Find out more

A Information gathering

Student B: look at the information in the table below and answer your partner's questions.

Activity	Time spent (1–10)	Average time spent in the UK over 80 years
Complaining		5 months
Doing housework		5.5 years
Eating		4 years
Laughing		3.5 months
Sleeping		26 years
Using a phone		4 years
Waiting in line		4.5 years
Watching TV		11 years
Working		11.5 years

Unit 7, page 51, Core vocabulary

C Word parts

Answers: words with *uni*

unified   uniform   universal   universe   university

Unit 7, page 54, Find out more

A Information gathering

Student B: use the table below. How many robots in movies and books can you name? Ask your partner for the missing information and complete the table.

Movie	Robot	Job/Purpose
Alien		
Star Wars	C-3PO	translator on a spaceship
Star Trek		
A.I. Artificial Intelligence	David	bought to replace dead son
Blade Runner		
Forbidden Planet	Robby the Robot	family servant and companion
RoboCop		
Transformers	Bumblebee	Sam's bodyguard
Godzilla		
Terminator	T-800	time traveler sent to kill a boy

Unit 8, page 59, Core vocabulary

C Word parts

Answers: words with *auto*

autobiography   autograph   automatic   automobile   autopilot

Unit 9, page 70, Find out more

Unit 9, page 70, Find out more

A Information gathering

Student B: use the table below. Ask your partner for the missing information and complete the table.

Animals and medical research		
Disease	**Animal used**	**Discovery**
Asthma	guinea pig	
Diabetes		insulin
Kidney failure	dog	
Polio	mouse	
Scarlet fever		penicillin
Smallpox		vaccine
Tetanus		vaccine

Unit 10, page 78, Find out more

A Information gathering

Student B: look at the information in the table below and answer your partner's questions. Then ask your partner for the missing information and complete the table.

Food production (in kilograms per person per year)					
Product	**China**	**France**	**Japan**	**UK**	**USA**
Chicken		17.8	10.9	22.2	54.6
Corn (maize)	144.3	240.5	0.0	0.0	
Cow	4.6	26.3		14.9	35.9
Cow's milk	27.6		59.1		284.2
Horse		0.1	0.0	0.1	0.2
Pig	38.6	32.0		12.1	28.3
Potato	66.1		18.6	97.5	61.8
Rice	151.6	2.0	66.4		26.8
Soybean	10.8	1.9	1.7	0.0	

Unit 11, page 83, Core vocabulary

C Word parts

Answers: words with *sur*

surcharge   surface   surname   surpassing   surplus

Unit 12, page 91, Core vocabulary

C Word parts

Answers: words with *inter*

interchangeable   interfere   international   internet   interstate

Unit 4, page 30, Find out more

A Information gathering

Student B: use the table below. Ask your partner for the missing information and complete the table.

Competition	Situation	Result
1 Apple v. Google	The iPhone was introduced in June 2007. Its first serious competitors in the smartphone market used Google's Android operating system, which was introduced in October 2008.	Smartphones have become the most common type of mobile phones in many countries. Android phones are nearly three times more common than Apple's iPhone.
2 Lewis Hamilton v. Nico Rosberg		
3 Scott v. Amundsen	Robert Scott was a British explorer. Roald Amundsen was a Norwegian explorer. Both arrived in Antarctica in 1911. They were competing to be the first to get to the South Pole.	Amundsen and his team won the race. They arrived on December 14, 1911. Scott arrived 33 days later. Scott and his team all died on the way back. Amundsen's team all made it back safely.
4 USSR v. USA space race		

Core vocabulary: keywords

Unit 1

assume

behavior

brand

income

industry

label

prevent

stock

trend

warn

Unit 2

award

benefit

blame

campaign

factor

mass

opportunity

promote

resource

technique

Unit 3

achieve

athlete

coach

complain

feature

further

seek

suggestion

typically

victim

Unit 4

bill

competition

deliver

increase

mention

observe

plus

rate

root

status

Unit 5

average

category

duty

growth

ignore

material

option

separate

solution

supply

Unit 6

divide

environmental

extend

gain

pension

principle

proposal

relative

schedule

survive

Unit 7

adopt

aid

career

code

doubt

effort

force

oppose

potential

serve

Unit 8

application

army

disease

equal

gun

replace

security

union

unlikely

waste

Unit 9

claim

contract

employee

examine

experiment

issue

parent

patient

refuse

training

Unit 10

accuse

basis

feed

generate

murder

prison

protection

release

suffer

suit

Unit 11

aware

contribution

debate

define

editor

legal

property

shift

survey

user

Unit 12

commit

despite

document

finance

host

penalty

refer

rely

source

vote

Alphabetical list

A

accuse
achieve
adopt
aid
application
army
assume
athlete
average
award
aware

B

basis
behavior
benefit
bill
blame
brand

C

campaign
career
category
claim
coach
code
commit
competition
complain
contract
contribution

D

debate
define
deliver
despite
disease
divide

document
doubt
duty

E

editor
effort
employee
environmental
equal
examine
experiment
extend

F

factor
feature
feed
finance
force
further

G

gain
generate
growth
gun

H

host

I

ignore
income
increase
industry
issue

L

label
legal

M

mass
material
mention
murder

O

observe
opportunity
oppose
option

P

parent
patient
penalty
pension
plus
potential
prevent
principle
prison
promote
property
proposal
protection

R

rate
refer
refuse
relative
release
rely
replace
resource
root

S

schedule
security

seek
separate
serve
shift
solution
source
status
stock
suffer
suggestion
suit
supply
survey
survive

T

technique
training
trend
typically

U

union
unlikely
user

V

victim
vote

W

warn
waste

Credits

In Focus 1

2024年1月20日　初版第1刷発行
2024年2月20日　初版第2刷発行

著　者　Charles Browne
　　　　Brent Culligan
　　　　Joseph Phillips

発行者　福　岡　正　人

発行所　株式会社　金　星　堂

（〒101-0051）東京都千代田区神田神保町 3-21
Tel　(03) 3263-3828〔営業部〕
　　　(03) 3263-3997〔編集部〕
Fax　(03) 3263-0716
https://www.kinsei-do.co.jp

編集担当　Richard Walker・Takahiro Imakado　　Printed in Japan
印刷所・製本所／シナノ書籍印刷株式会社

ISBN978-4-7647-4193-5　　C1082